REVISED EDITION IV.

YOU CAN GROW ORCHIDS

By **MARY NOBLE**

Paintings by
Marion Ruff Sheehan

Published by:

Mary Noble McQuerry, Jacksonville, Florida

Fourth Edition, Third Printing 1983
Produced in U.S.A.
ISBN-0-913928-04-6

DEDICATION: To Fred B. Noble, 1883-1978

CONTENTS

The Cover: Cattleya violacea

YOUR INVITATION TO GROW ORCHIDS 5
Everybody is doing it!

I. STRUCTURE OF PLANTS AND FLOWERS 9
How orchids are put together

II. CULTURE 33
Coordinate the elements of the environment

III. POTTING 47
Your choice of materials and containers

IV. THE ORCHIDS 57
Infinite variety in colors, sizes and shapes

V. PROPAGATION 101
How to multiply your plants

VI. PROBLEMS 113
Pests, diseases and how to cope with them

VII. HOUSING 121
Greenhouses, windowsills, orchids indoors and out

VIII. CORSAGES AND ARRANGEMENTS 127
Enjoy your orchids

Index 134

ACKNOWLEDGEMENTS: Sketches, Marion R. Sheehan and Bruno Alberts; Floral designs, Mrs. Truman Green, Mrs. J. Frank McClain, Mrs. Winona W. Jordan, Mrs. Clif C. Curry.

PHOTOS by the author and Jack McQuerry, Louis O. Egner, Lewis Ellsworth, Lewis C. Vaughn, Ray Stafford, and D. C. Flynn.

Cattleya Grand Tetons has eight-inch white blooms. Cattleyas are the most familiar orchids but there are thousands of other types that you can grow.

YOUR INVITATION
TO GROW ORCHIDS

This book is for you if you know nothing about orchids and do not have your first plant—yet.

It is for you if you are a beginner with a little knowledge and a wish for more.

It is for you if you are a dirt gardener who likes to watch things grow.

Or if you are an indoor gardener who wants to live with live plants and have exotic flowers year round.

Orchid growing is the most fascinating hobby in the world.

YOU can grow orchids. Anybody can.

But why should you?

For fun. The orchid family is the most fascinating plant family of all. The flowers are the most highly developed of all flowers. So this is the most challenging of flower hobbies. There's something in it to interest everybody, so your whole family can participate.

For flowers. You may think of orchids as only purple or white. This is only the beginning. There are soft pinks, bright greens, rich golds, reds, yellows, and gorgeous blues . . . any color except black. There are black markings on some flowers, but no all-black orchid bloom.

There are flowers in sizes running from infinitesimal to exhibition hybrids almost a foot wide. The shapes are astonishing. Some flowers look like butterflies, others like spiders, ballet dancers or nesting doves. There are types to please any taste, bizarre or beautiful. You might want to specialize in miniatures, tiny plants with tiny flowers to grow on a windowsill.

Furthermore, since there are some orchids which bloom at each of the four seasons, by selecting plants with assorted blooming times you can have flowers around the calendar. Even a dozen plants with different habits will give you an almost continuous flower show.

For relaxation. If you think orchids take time, you are right. Because if you grow them, you will spend time with them. But orchids are tough and you can keep them going with a minimum of attention when you are busy.

But in this age of hustle and stress, there is no better therapy for yourself than a few hours in the greenhouse or working with orchid houseplants. The time you spend with your orchids will do more for you than it does for the plants. Working with plants relieves tensions and takes out the kinks better than having your back rubbed.

Throw away your tranquilizers!

A Popular Hobby

A few people were growing orchids 150 years ago, but until recently this was a hobby only for the rich. Plants were expensive, so was equipment, and information was scarce.

Those of us who have been orchid growers for 30 years or more are pioneers. But now there are hobby growers by the thousands.

Four things have contributed to the astonishing increase in amateur orchid growers in recent years.

One, the mass production of orchid plants. This was brought about by the discovery in 1922 of a better method for germinating orchid seed, which resulted in commercial growers having more plants than they needed (or could take care of) for their cut flower trade. Mass production made plants easily available and brought prices within reach of average gardeners.

Two, the mass production of prefabricated greenhouses. Greenhouse manufacturers now make handsome small houses which fit suburban back yards and suburban budgets. Now a greenhouse is a status symbol, just like a swimming pool. Everybody in the neighborhood wants one. You can get an attractive prefabricated greenhouse for less than $1,000.

However, many hobbyists are growing orchids in apartments or condominiums, in the suburbs without greenhouses, or indoors under artificial lights.

Three, the great interest in plants of all kinds, plus the need for "at home" hobbies that provide entertainment without long drives to recreational areas.

Four, the increased availability of information. As more people grow orchids they share their knowledge with their friends. People are learning that an orchid plant in bloom might cost no more than a fine amaryllis bulb, that it might need less attention than a rose bush, and be as durable as a philodendron. Information increases confidence.

This book is one of many, most others more advanced, on orchid growing, and the fact that the first three editions sold more than 50,000 copies world-wide tells you about the interest in orchids.

There are a number of fine magazines published by orchid societies, national or regional, to help you.

This is your invitation to join us in the orchid fraternity.

You need three qualification: a genuine interest in these flowers and plants, a willingness to learn more and more about them, and a lively curiosity about new developments.

Orchid growing is an enchanting hobby. If you live to be a hundred, you won't begin to see all the orchids already in existence, and new ones are blooming every day. Further, every grower has his own way of growing his plants, and new techniques and materials are constantly being developed. So you will never know all there is to know. You can forever learn something new and interesting.

No attempt is made here to mention all the different kinds of orchids. There are thousands. Our remarks pertain to the major cultivated kinds, with specific mention of only a few in each group. You will find many, many orchids not included that you will want in your collection.

A Bit of Advice

However, you must understand from the beginning that orchids have certain requirements, which may be quite different from other plants that you grow. And you must tend to their needs. Mere survival isn't sufficient. You want the best growth and the finest flowers of which your plants are capable.

Two notes of caution to you, as a beginner. One, start with blooming size plants of whatever types you choose that are suitable for the environment you can offer. Later, when you become experienced, you can grow seedlings. But seedlings are babies and naturally more tender than mature plants. And why begin a hobby with plants too small to bloom for one or more years? Plants in bud or in bloom are not expensive, depending on the type and the quality, and it is best to begin with those on which flowers are open or imminent.

Do not be misled by advertisements which tell you you will get rich quick by growing orchids. It can't be done. And beware of bargains that are too much cheaper than plants of the same nature offered by other growers.

Always buy from established, reliable companies, and do not begin with newly imported plants. Again, when you are experienced you might import some plants and re-establish them after fumigation, travel and climate changes. But begin with plants grown in your own country that can be sold to you established in pots and in active growth.

And don't be dismayed at orchid names. Through this text we have scattered simple prounciations. And as you acquire your plants and take care of them, their names will become easy, like the names of your friends.

If you come across unfamiliar words in this book, consult the glossary in YOU CAN GROW CATTLEYA ORCHIDS.

CHAPTER I

STRUCTURE OF PLANTS AND FLOWERS

For you to become acquainted with an orchid plant, it is important that you know something about its structure, behavior and habits.

An orchid plant is not fragile nor delicate. On the contrary, it is tough and strong.

This is a plant that has struggled to survive in nature, and has won out in competition with other tropical plants which are gigantic in size by comparison. The orchid in the wilderness manages to get its share of sunlight, rain, and air by taking to branches high up in the trees, growing on rocks in exposed places, often within reach of spray from waterfalls or moisture from fogs and low clouds.

Some orchid plants look like succulents because of their thick leaves. Some are equipped to store up reserves of food and moisture to carry them through dry seasons. This reserve helps your plants survive if you neglect them, but it cannot sustain them forever.

But you do not want your orchids to be neglected or mistreated. Neither do you want to kill them with kindness. This is the mistake most beginners make, particularly by watering their plants too much.

So, if you understand how your orchid plants are put together, you will know better how to keep them happy.

Slipper orchids are in great favor. This is a handsome hybrid, Paphiopedilum Ernest Read.

Basically the structure of an orchid plant is the same as any other plant, for it has roots, stems, leaves and flowers. But these parts are adapted to its way of life, and therefore differ somewhat from the same parts of other plants which you grow in your garden.

Most of the orchids in cultivation are epiphytes. That is, they do not grow in the ground, but instead grow in trees or rocks above ground level. This puts the roots out into the air, and the word epiphyte means air plant, or literally "to grow upon a plant." Epiphytes (pronounced "EP-e-fights") are not parasites, and epiphytes do not feed on the host trees. Mistletoe, for example, is a parasite which grows on trees and takes food from them. Orchids are epiphytes which grow upon trees but do not derive any support from them. Orchids get their nourishment from rain, dust and debris that comes their way.

Cymbidiums and others are terrestrials, which means "to grow in the ground," in a method more like that of garden plants. But cymbidiums have certain requirements, so you can't just dig a hole and plant them along with your daffodils, even though they are terrestrials.

Most of our native U.S. orchids are terrestrials that grow in forests and fields although there are a number of native epiphytes in Florida.

Sympodial Orchid Plants

Many orchids have a habit of growing that is called sympodial ("sim-PO-dee-al").

This is entirely different from most garden plants. For instance, a shrub has a single main stem or trunk. As it grows, it branches up and out from this main stem, growing from terminal growth buds at the ends of the branches or twigs. It grows upward.

A sympodial orchid does just the opposite. It does not branch out from a stem, but puts up another growth just like the one before. The new growth has its beginning at the base of the newest existing bulb. It grows sideways.

Generally a plant produces one new growth (pseudobulb) each year, but a plant of several pseudobulbs may make several new growths simultaneously, and hybrids may have two or more cycles of growth in a year.

Cattleyas are sympodial in habit. So are cymbidiums, brassavolas, laelias, epidendrums, oncidiums, odontoglossums and dendrobiums, to name a few.

Rarely does one bulb constitute a self-sufficient plant. The growing bulb draws on reserves of the previous bulbs for strength. Therefore, on a cattleya, for example, it is desirable to have four

CATTLEYA ORCHID PLANT
(SYMPODIAL TYPE)

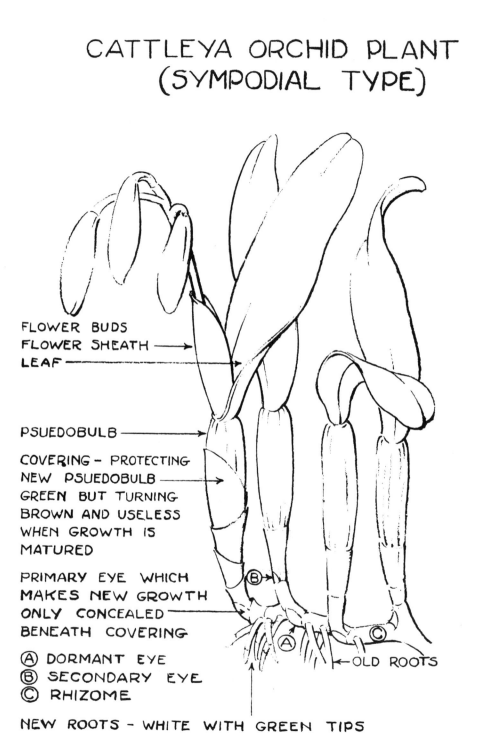

FLOWER BUDS
FLOWER SHEATH
LEAF

PSUEDOBULB

COVERING – PROTECTING
NEW PSUEDOBULB
GREEN BUT TURNING
BROWN AND USELESS
WHEN GROWTH IS
MATURED

PRIMARY EYE WHICH
MAKES NEW GROWTH
ONLY CONCEALED
BENEATH COVERING

Ⓐ DORMANT EYE
Ⓑ SECONDARY EYE
Ⓒ RHIZOME

OLD ROOTS

NEW ROOTS – WHITE WITH GREEN TIPS

BRUNO ALBERTS

or more mature bulbs to support each growing bulb, and essential to have at least two or three. A few orchids, such as some catasetums, cycnoches, mormodes can get along with only one mature bulb to support a new lead.

There are five major parts of a sympodial orchid plant.

RHIZOME — The base of the plant is a hard, woody stem called a rhizome (rhymes with "home" and is pronounced "RYE-zom") which is the coupling or connecting link between the upright sections (pseudobulbs) of the plant. The rhizome creeps along on top or just below the surface of the potting medium. In most cattleyas it is about an inch long between bulbs and roughly the thickness of a pencil or a little finger. On some orchids such as oncidiums and cymbidiums the bulbs are so close together that the rhizome is not visible.

PSEUDOBULB — The stem which rises from the rhizome and is between the rhizome and the leaf is called the pseudobulb ("SUE-doe-bulb"). "Pseudo" means "false" because this is not really a bulb although it functions like one. The pseudobulb acts as a storage place for moisture and food, and makes it possible for the plant to live in a climate where there is a lengthy dry season. (This doesn't mean you should let your plants go without water, but only that in nature some of them have to manage for months on dew and mist without any great amount of rain.)

The size and shape of the pseudobulb varies with the genus and species. (See illustrations.) On many cattleya hybrids the pseudobulb is about the length of a man's hand from fingertip to wrist, and about as thick as three of his fingers. Large plants may have bulbs half again as high and wider in proportion, whereas some of the sophronitis hybrids have bulbs only two or three inches tall.

Pseudobulbs take different shapes on different orchids. Cattleya guttata makes tall, slender bulbs that may be three feet tall and not much bigger around than pencils. Epidendrum atropurpureum has bulbs about the size and shape of hen's eggs. Oncidium ampliatum has round flat bulbs like turtles in a heap. The various dendrobiums have tall, slender upright bulbs, cascading canes or small oval bulbs.

Paphiopedilums are sympodial but do not have pseudobulbs.

LEAF — The leaf which comes singly, in pairs or multiple numbers varies from plant to plant. Most cattleyas have one leaf which grows upright from the top of the bulb, but types with two or more leaves horizontally at the same position are called bifoliates. Cymbidiums have several pairs of long narrow leaves which arch gracefully upward from the sides of each bulb. Some oncidiums and brassavolas have round terete leaves. Stanhopeas have broad veined leaves.

The size, shape, color and substance of orchid leaves vary so greatly that it is difficult to realize some plants are of the same family. Some are dark and leathery, others are small and fragile. But all have the usual function of a leaf, the process of photosynthesis, which is the manufacture of starch and sugar by the chlorophyll in the presence of light using nutrients, gasses and water that have been absorbed by roots and foliage. Photosynthesis is the process on which we depend for the oxygen we breathe, which is a by-product given off into the air by the foliage.

Most orchids are evergreen but a few are deciduous and shed their leaves in the dormant season. Leaves on old back bulbs fall as new growths develop on the front and draw on the reserves in the back pseudobulbs. Roots at the back die off and in time the pseudobulbs shrivel and die.

SHEATH — A cattleya has a green sheath growing out of the top of the pseudobulb next to the leaf. It is about the size and shape of a knife blade. This is the protective covering for the buds while they are very small. Bulb, leaf and sheath all reach maturity at about the same time. A growth on a mature plant which does not make a sheath is called "blind" and probably will not flower. Seedlings seldom make sheaths until they are near flowering size.

On other sympodial orchids the sheath may be smaller and perhaps almost hidden between two leaves. Some sympodial plants do not have sheaths, and some bloom from the base of the bulb.

ROOTS — The roots grow from the rhizome. They are white and fleshy with a spongy covering layer. Roots absorb water and nutrients for the plant.

SYMPODIAL TYPE ORCHID PLANTS

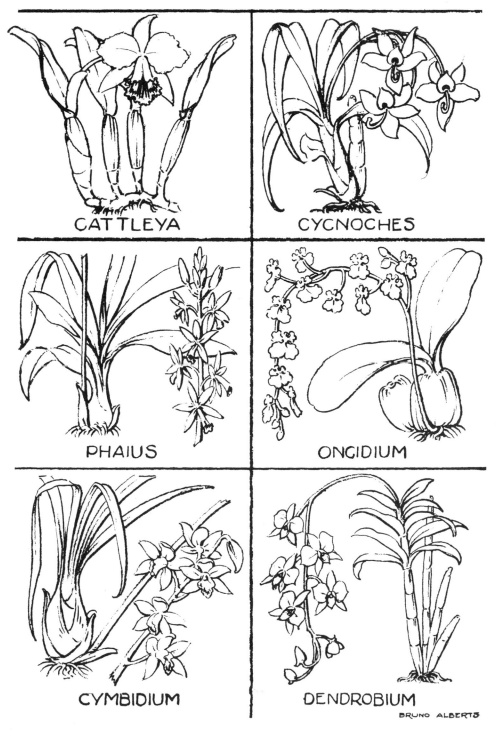

CATTLEYA

CYCNOCHES

PHAIUS

ONCIDIUM

CYMBIDIUM

DENDROBIUM

BRUNO ALBERTS

VANDA ORCHID PLANT
(MONOPODIAL TYPE)

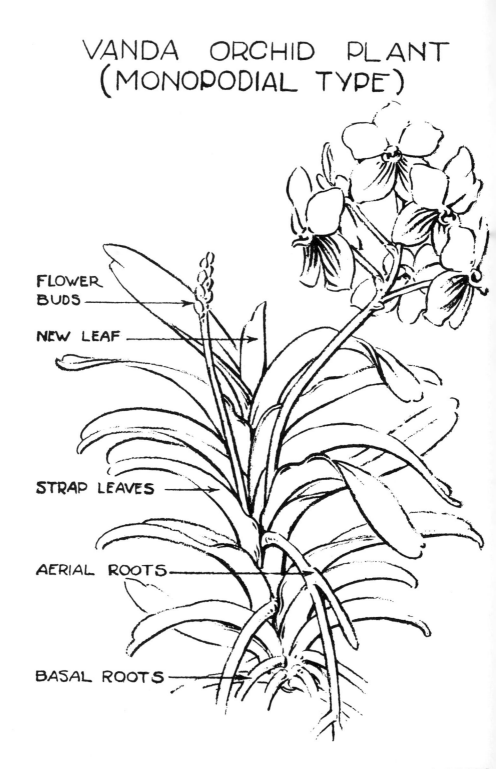

FLOWER BUDS

NEW LEAF

STRAP LEAVES

AERIAL ROOTS

BASAL ROOTS

BRUNO ALBERTS

Roots weave through the potting medium and travel round and round inside the pot, sometimes hang over the edge. On a sympodial orchid, roots on the back end of the plant may cease to function as new roots grow on the front. Brown, dry roots may be cut off at repotting time. New roots are white with green tips. Orchids planted on logs will wrap roots around and snugly attach them to the wood as holdfasts for security. This is the way they stay on the trees in nature, in spite of high winds.

Monopodial Orchid Plants

Entirely different from sympoliad growth is the growth of a monopodial orchid plant. Monopodial means "one foot" whereas sympodial indicates several stems. Pronounce it "mono-PO-dee-al."

A monopodial orchid has neither rhizomes nor pseudobulbs. It does not make repetitious growths. Instead it makes continuous growth upward from the top of the plant.

STEM — The single center support of a monopodial orchid may be a visible stem, as in a reed-stem epidendrum, or a stem hidden by the leaves as in a strapleaf vanda.

The plant grows continuously taller, and in some monopodial orchids may be 10 to 12 feet tall, as in the arachnis, renantheras and terete vandas when grown to perfection outdoors as they are in Malaya and Hawaii.

LEAVES — Quite in contrast to the foliage habit of a sympodial orchid, a monopodial orchid generally has leaves alternately or in pairs the entire length of the stem. Lower leaves may fall as the plant gets taller.

Leaves take quite different shapes. On the strapleaf vandas they are like green ribbons, placed in rather arching positions. On terete vandas the pencil-slim stems and the roundish blunt horizontal proturberances that are the leaves look about alike. Angraecums have leathery strap leaves. Small thick leaves line the tall stems of arachnis and renantheras. Phalaenopsis have broad graceful glossy leaves.

ROOTS — Aerial roots are produced at intervals along the stem, and grow outward and down into the air or the potting medium. Roots may cascade for considerable distances, and if a plant is grown in a basket, the roots may extend for some distance out of the bottom. Dry or dead roots look like brown strings. Active roots are whitish with green tips.

FLOWERS — A monopodial orchid plant does not have flower sheaths, but it produces spikes of flowers from the main stem between two leaves or from the base of the plant. In some types the flower spikes may be quite long. Several spikes may be produced simultaneously by a large plant.

Since a monopodial orchid has no pseudobulbs, it has no reserve of moisture and therefore needs watering more frequently than a sympodial orchid. A monopodial orchid is not likely to take a definite rest period, although growth may be in spurts and may be noticeably slower in the winter or dry months.

A phalaenopsis is a familiar example of monopodial growth. The plant is composed of broad flat leaves, perhaps two on a seedling, several on an old plant. As new leaves mature, older ones at the base may fall off, but the plant never gets very tall. Flower spikes may originate at the base just above the potting medium, or from between the leaves.

How the Plant Grows

A sympodial orchid plant makes successive growths and each complete growth (rhizome, pseudobulb, leaf, sheath) represents a cycle. Monopodial orchids do not have such well-defined cycles, but growth and flowering may develop with reasonable regularity.

The growth pattern goes like this:

THE EYE: In its embryonic state, the new bulb is visible on most sympodial orchids at the base of the newest completed pseudobulb.

MONOPODIAL TYPE ORCHID PLANTS

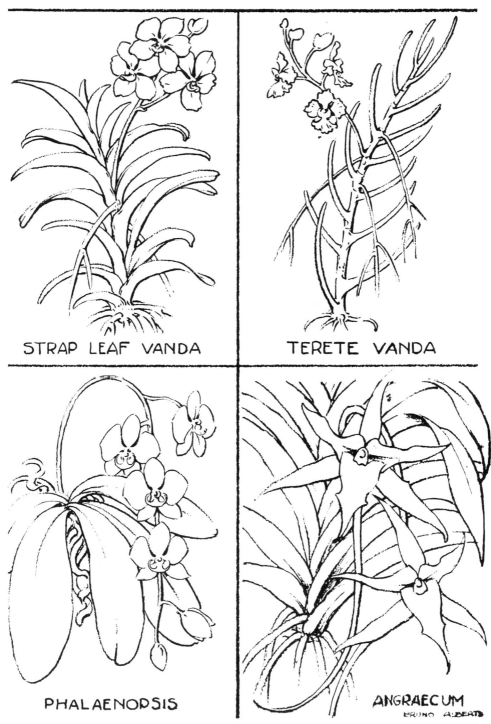

STRAP LEAF VANDA

TERETE VANDA

PHALAENOPSIS

ANGRAECUM

BRUNO ALBERTS

On a cattleya it appears as a little triangular shaped bump right where the bulb curves upward from the rhizome. It is called an eye. Generally there are two eyes on opposite sides of the bulb, and there may be a third, or reserve, eye slightly higher on the bulb. This one won't grow except in an emergency if something happens to the two primary eyes. Perhaps only one of the primary eyes will develop, but if the plant is vigorous and well-grown, both may make new bulbs. (See sketch.)

On other sympodial orchids the eye is similar, and located at the base of the bulb. Generally it is covered by a brown papery protective covering, and if you are removing this covering to check plants for scale (which often attacks and kills the eyes), or to see if your plant has a good green eye, take care, as you can very easily pull off the eye when removing the cover.

Sometimes good eyes on back bulbs will grow of their own accord, or they may be stimulated to grow by removing the back bulbs from the active front bulbs. (See Propagation.)

Monopodial orchids have eyes, too, but they are not so easy to see. And the vegetative eyes along the stem may remain dormant unless something unusual stimulates them into growth. For instance, if the top of a vanda is broken, it will probably make keikis (baby plants) from eyes somewhere along the stem, and this is one way to propagate monopodial plants.

Phaleanopsis plants sometimes make new plants from unseen eyes at the base, and these eyes, too, sometimes can be activated by removing the top of a leggy plant.

THE LEAD — When a cattleya begins to grow, the eye swells up and pushes outward from the mature pseudobulb. It grows horizontally for probably an inch, forming the new section of the rhizome, which eventually becomes woody. Then it turns upward and grows parallel to the previous pseudobulb, and is called a lead until the growth is mature. (See sketches of growth cycle in "You Can Grow Cattleya Orchids.")

A new growth on a cymbidium appears as a sturdy, green, roundish growth pointing upward at a slight outward angle from the base of the mature bulb. After it gets several inches tall it begins to differentiate into leaves, which gradually grow longer and taller as growth progresses.

A new growth on a paphiopedilum appears like a green plant right beside the last mature growth or between its lower leaves.

A new plant on a monopodial orchid, such as a strapleaf vanda which may make a new plant from somewhere along the stem, looks like a well-formed miniature plant which increases in size and number of leaves as it grows.

THE BULB — As the lead on a cattleya grows, it is almost flat, and the bulb does not begin to plump up noticeably until the lead has almost reached its height and the leaf has unfolded.

While the bulbs are growing, the outer covering, if any, is green, and on maturity of the growth it turns brown and may be peeled off, or left alone if scale is not a problem.

THE FLOWER SHEATH — As noted, not all sympodial, and no monopodial orchids have flower sheaths. On those that do, notably of the cattleya alliance, the flower sheath develops with the lead, so that when the bulb reaches its mature height and the leaf unfolds, the tip of the sheath can be seen. When growth is completed, the flower sheath is in position at the top of the pseudobulb adjacent to the leaf.

The spray orchids put up flower spikes which may be as thin as fine wire, as on some oncidiums, or thick robust spikes as on cymbidiums. Individual buds are not apparent until the spike reaches some length, when it may branch. Individual flowers usually open a few at a time, but on many spray orchids eventually the entire spike is in bloom at once.

Flower Production

The time of flowering depends upon one or more factors: inheritance, temperature, daylength, plant habit and growth habit.

For example, cymbidiums set their buds during the long days of summer, which means flower spikes develop during the fall and winter and bloom in the spring. Night temeprature affects bud

Phalaenopsis sumatrana, a species, has cinnamon stripes and is a parent of many yellow and spotted Phalaenopsis hybrids.

initiation, which makes it difficult to flower cymbidiums in hot climates unless there is artificial cooling or sufficient altitude to drop the temperature within suitable range.

Each cattleya species has a definite time of bloom, which is related to conditions in its native habitat, but the flowering season of hybrids may be variable and frequent.

For instance, in nature Cattleya mossiae grows during the summer rainy season, completes bulb, leaf, sheath, and then does nothing during the winter. The sheath, completed the previous year, produces flowers in the spring.

Cattleya warscewiczii (synonym C. gigas), on the other hand, begins a new growth in the spring and flowers immediately in early sumer before the pseudobulb is fully mature.

Such species need definite periods of rest.

But hybrids, which are combinations of species (now into many generations removed from the first crosses), may flower at either or both seasons and may grow constantly.

Phalaenopsis generally bloom in the spring, but when spikes are cut after flowers open, many of them will make secondary spikes of flowers. It is important to leave a portion of the old flower stem, and to cut just above a plump node. Cool nights initiate buds.

The sympodial orchids generally flower only on the new growths, although some cattleya type hybrids may flower from a sheath that has been dormant for a few months as well as on a new bulb that is just maturing. But cattleyas do not flower a second time from a pseudobulb. Dendrobium phalaenopsis, on the other hand, frequently bloom from old and new bulbs year after year.

The monopodial orchids move upward in their flowering, producing spikes from higher along the stem between the leaves.

Those orchids which have definite seasons of flowering, followed or preceded by definite seasons of rest or inactivity, should be treated according to their wishes. For instance, Dendrobium nobile types need a period of chilling and comparative dryness in the fall to encourage flowering. Oncidium splendidum flowers best if kept rather dry in the fall after the growths are made up. More about this in the section on Watering.

The Parts of a Flower

Orchids are highly developed flowers. They take on many different shapes, sizes and colors but the basic structure is the same whether it is a fat-faced paphiopedilum, a butterfly-like oncidium or a spidery brassia.

SEPALS — On most of our garden flowers the sepals are rather inconspicuous. Examine a rose. The sepals are the little green points that cover the bud when it is small but they do not progress as the flower enlarges. When the rose opens, the little green sepals are hidden beneath the petals at the top of the stem.

On an orchid, the sepals are included in the showy part of the flower. When the flower is a closed bud, the three sepals form the outside of the bud and the petals are curled up inside.

When the orchid opens, it appears to have six petals, but three of them are sepals. They generally are narrower than the petals and alternate with the petals in the flower design. If in doubt, examine the flower from the back. The sepals are lower on the stem than the petals.

Sometimes the basic flower parts vary. In a paphiopedilum the top or dorsal sepal is wider than the petals, the two other sepals are joined together behind the pouch (lip).

PETALS — Of the three petals on an orchid, two are alike and placed horizontally. They are generally wider than the sepals, but not in all types of orchids, and often the same color and pattern. In

A — Cattleya
B — Paphiopedilum
C — Miltonia
D — Cymbidium
E — Oncidium
F — Vanda
G — Phalaenopsis

1. Sepals
2. Petals
3. Lip
4. Column
5. Bud
6. Sheath

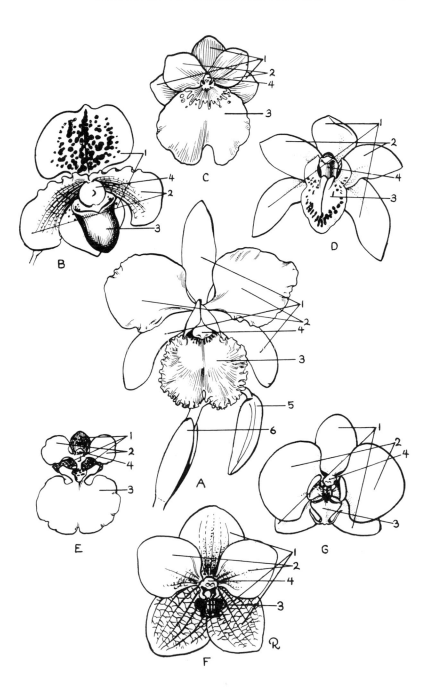

phalaenopsis, cattleyas and cymbidiums the sepals and petals are usually of similar color and the petals are wider. In oncidiums and paphs the petals may be quite different in color and pattern from the sepals. See sketches of flower parts.

LIP — The third petal is often the most spectacular part of the orchid flower and is called the lip or labellum. Rich veining and brilliant color may characterize this segment. It may be fluted or fringed. It is larger or smaller and sometimes different in color, shape and design from the other two petals or the sepals.

There are numerous variations. On a "slipper orchid" the lip is the slipper. On a "dancing lady" orchid, the lip is the ballet skirt. But on a vanda the lip is much smaller than the other segments but often more brightly colored.

The lip is the distinguishing mark of an orchid. Most flowers have petals all alike, but an orchid always has two matching petals and one that is different.

The lip is often ingenious in design. Its color is designed to lead the pollinating insect to the column, where the pollen is. It often provides a landing place for a flying insect. In some orchids, the lip traps the insect in such a way that he has to pass by the column to pick up or deposit pollen. When a bee is attracted to a flower of Coryanthes macrantha, for instance, he lands and scratches where the odor is, but invariably falls into the bucket-shaped part of the lip which the flower has partly filled with water. To get out, he must crawl through a tunnel, thus passing the column and picking up or depositing pollen.

COLUMN — The column contains the reproductive organs. On most flowers the stamens and pistils are separate parts, but in an orchid they are fused into one part.

The column appears in the center of the flower, with the sepals and petals surrounding it, and is at the apex of all six parts. In a cattleya-type orchid the lip usually folds over top of the column, which may be called the tube, with the portion below the column called the throat.

The column is a complex structure which both disburses and receives pollen. But in most orchids it is designed so the orchid

Brassia bidens. This green and brown spider orchid has narrow sepals and petals and a large spotted lip.

cannot pollinate itself, and the pollinating insect who brings pollen will deposit it and then pick up fresh pollen on his way out.

Drawings of the columns with identification of the parts, and sketches on how to pollinate these orchids are to be found in the other books in this series.

Orchid Names

Orchid names are easy when you get accustomed to them.

The plant family is the Orchidaceae, pronounced "or-kid-DAY-see-ee." The family includes all the orchids of whatever type, but not such unrelated plants as bauhinias, which are called orchid trees but are no kin. You will seldom use the botanical family name, but may refer to "the Orchid Family."

Within the family are many genera, some 600 or more. Genera is plural for genus. Genera is pronounced "JEN-er-ah" and genus is pronounced "GEE-nus."

The related genera are grouped into botanical tribes but you need not be concerned with tribes.

In an orchid name, the genus names comes first. Cattleya is a genus. So is Oncidium, Dendrobium, Phaius, Cymbidium, Phalaenopsis, Odontoglossum, Lycaste and many more. The genus name may be abbreviated once it is established which genus is being discussed.

So when you refer to Cattleya trianaei, Cattleya, the genus name, comes first. Then comes trianaei, which is the species name. A species is a member of a genus. There are some estimated 20,000 species of orchids within the estimated 600 genera. Species is pronounced "SPE-sees." (The word is both singular and plural. There is no such thing as a specie, it is a species.)

Orchids are sort of like the Chinese people. Their last names (group names) come first.

The species are plants as originated in nature, even if they are now propagated in cultivation.

Hybrids may be made by nature, but most of the orchid hybrids have been made by man. A hybrid name looks just the same as a species name, to an extent. First comes the genus, and then the hybrid. For instance, a hybrid with Cattleya warscewiczii (gigas) and Cattleya mossiae as parents (both species) is Cattleya Enid. The species name begins with a small letter, the genus and hybrid names with capitals.

The name of a hybrid is called a collective epithet. It is a name which applies to every seedling that resulted from the cross, and to all future seedlings of the same cross.

But this is only the beginning, because orchids of one genus will hybridize with orchids of another genus. This makes a bigeneric hybrid. Not all plants or animals will do this.

Birds mate only with their own kind. You never see a bluejay with a red head because one parent was a woodpecker. Dogs, however, mix types so well that some are of unidentifiable ancestry. Orchids are like dogs. Therefore, you might say the progeny of two purebred cocker spaniels is still a cocker spaniel, so two Cattleyas produce Cattleya offspring.

But mate a cocker spaniel with a dachshund and you have a mixed breed. Hybridize a Laelia with a Cattleya and you have a bigeneric hybrid, a Laeliocattleya.

Bigeneric hybrids in orchids are just the beginning, as there are multigeneric plants with several genera in their background. And whereas this type of mixed breed is not desirable in a dog, it is often a show winner among orchids.

It is this ability of orchids to hybridize across generic lines that is producing such fascinating flowers. And since there are already an uncounted number of hybrids and new ones coming along every day, the variation and enchantment within the Orchid Family are unbelievable and limitless.

We are getting new generic names all the time, too, as combinations are made for the first time. Over 200 genera are included in the published list of hybrids at this writing, and others are constantly being added. This need not frighten you. You need learn only the names that interest you as you make the acquaintance of the flowers.

The originator who produces and first flowers a new hybrid may name it and register it with The Royal Horticultural Society, London, the International Registration Authority for Orchids. Anyone else must have the originator's permission to register a cross. But once a hybrid is named, every repeat of the same parentage has this same name (collective epithet.) Thus, every plant that results from a cross of Cattleya Bow Bells and Cattleya Joyce Hannington is named Cattleya Madeleine Knowlton, whether or not the same two plants of C. Bow Bells and C. Joyce Hannington were used as parents when the cross was remade. Each time a Phalaenopsis Suemid and a Phalaenopsis Ruby Lips are used together as parents the progeny all are Phalaenopsis Jack McQuerry because this is the registered name for this combination.

Next we come to the variety or cultivar names. There may be literally thousands of plants produced from one seed pod, all with the same name. To distinguish certain ones (usually those of unusual merit) the owner may give different plants variety or cultivar names to distinguish them from their brothers and sisters. Thus if you have three plants of Cattleya trianaei you might call one 'Tom,' another 'Dick' and the third 'Harry.' But every time you divide your plant of Cattleya trianaei 'Tom' each piece of it is still 'Tom.' This is the way good vegetative divisions of fine plants are distinguished, and in time there may be many plants of C. trianaei 'Tom' in existence. Variety or cultivar names (the terms are synonymous) are set apart in single quotes: Cymbidium Alexanderi 'Westonbirt.' In our collection we use Clone A, B or C to distinguish different plants of the same cross, and Division #1, #2, #3 to identify divisions of Clone A or whatever.

Meristem plants should carry identification of the clone in a varietal name as all mericlones are vegetative divisions of certain plants, and more than one clone of a cross may be meristemmed. Example: Blc. Norman's Bay 'Low' and Blc. Norman's Bay 'Hercules' have both been propagated by meristemming and many plants of each are available.

A plant that receives an award, must be assigned a varietal name to identify the particular clone.

About awards. Various orchid organizations give awards to outstanding flowers or plants which then become as a title to the winning clone. Thus you may see Paphiopedilum Maudiae 'Magnificum' FCC/RHS because this clone was awarded a First Class Certificate in 1901. There are many divisions of Paph. Maudiae 'Magnificum' FCC/RHS avalaible today from divisions made through the years.

Paphiopedilum Maudiae "Magnificum" FCC/RHS, a famous green and white slipper orchid.

Eigteen other clones of Paph. Maudiae have received various awards since that time. The award is carried by all divisions and mericlones of a plant, but not by seedlings made by crossing this plant with another.

Other award initials you see are AM for Award of Merit, HCC for High Class Certificate, and the various awards for culture and botanical merit. Society initials are AOS for American Orchid Society, RHS for Royal Horticultural Society, AOC for Australian Orchid Council, and others.

A vertical arrangement of Kenilworth ivy, white phalaenopsis and white cattleyas in an antique milk glass bottle on a footed teak base. Arranged by Mrs. Truman Green.

CHAPTER II

CULTURE

Orchids are different — not difficult.

Your orchids will do their best to adapt themselves to the conditions you provide for them. But you must try your best to give them an environment that meets their needs.

Orchids do not need to be coddled. You can kill them with kindness.

The important thing is that you understand what your plants want, and that you give them the attention that helps them grow and flower to their best potential.

Temperature, light, ventilation, water and fertilizer are the essential ingredients.

The secret of success is a balance among all these ingredients.

Temperature

Most orchids are happy in temperatures that are comfortable for people. If the air in your house or greenhouse feels good to you, it is probably suitable for your plants.

Some people think that because most of the epiphytic orchids come from the tropics, they should be grown in hot, damp air.

But if you have been to the tropics you know it can get very cold at night, especially in the higher altitudes. Darjeeling is in the north of India and within sight of Mt. Everest. There are 600 orchid species native in a broad area and the climate is far from hot. The mists that drench the plants with moisture are icy. Orchids grow all over the world but many of the cultivated kinds are tropicals which like it warm by day and cooler at night. A difference between day and night temperatures is essential.

Lower temperature at night slows down the plants' respiration which in turn increases their growth.

In the early days of orchid growing, there were three houses: the cool house, the intermediate house and the stove house. Now we know that many (but not all) types of orchids can be grown together in a small greenhouse or on a window sill.

Minimum temperatures, where suggested, indicate the desirable range. However, many plants can survive lower temperatures for brief periods and emerge relatively unscathed from a period when the heat goes off. Some have been known to collapse completely under such conditions, while plants in adjoining pots survived, none the worse.

As to higher temperatures, heat needs to be accompanied by higher humidity and moving air. Dry heat dehydrates plants, but warm moist air is desirable. If you live in a desert, or a hot dry climate, you must have cooling equipment and insulation to lower the temperature.

Science reports show that ordinary garden plants begin to grow at about 40°, increase to the optimum of 84°, then slow down and cease to grow at about 100°. Different plants have varying optimum ranges, and many orchids thrive between 75° and 95°. Growth may cease at lower or higher temperatures.

Most orchids do well if the minimum is about 55°F. but our plants have endured lower temperatures. The danger lies in damage to flowers or buds.

Temperatures too high can be as detrimental as those too low. Some plants find high temperatures very trying because the heat causes moisture to evaporate faster than the roots can take it up, and they go into semidormancy during hot seasons.

For example, vandas and related plants grow wonderfully well in Southeast Asia, but cattleyas do not perform as well there as in cooler climates. Cymbidiums do extremely well in Southern California but are more difficult to flower in Florida because the night temperatures are too high in late summer for buds to initiate easily.

Many growers use cooling equipment in their greenhouses to temper heat and dryness, or to grow cool orchids in hot climates. Small coolers are no more of a luxury than small heaters for greenhouses, and if you have both you can give your orchids nearly ideal conditions.

Home air conditioners take moisture out of the air. They modify the temperature for orchids, but require that humidity be increased. Wet-pad type coolers, on the other hand, add moisture as they cool.

Light

Orchid plants need sunlight. Light is used to turn moisture and nutrients into plant growth. A good rule is to give your plants as much light as they can stand without scorching.

Cattleya plants that are a beautiful dark green color are handsome but may not flower, as they are probably not receiving enough light. The most productive cattleyas are light green bordering on a yellowish-green.

Remember that in nature most orchids grow high in the treetops, and if trees are deciduous the orchids may be exposed to full sun at certain seasons. Bear in mind, too, that up high like that the air is moving constantly, and there is moisture in mist and dew and so the hot sun is not a dry sun, and it is tempered by the atmosphere.

Too much sunlight is indicated by scorched spots on the foliage or pseudobulbs. The spot may be lighter at first, then turn darker, like an iron scorch on a piece of silk. Rarely does it discolor an entire plant, only the portion of the leaf or bulb that is hit by strong direct rays.

Actually, the burn damage is caused by the plant tissue getting too hot. If a leaf feels hot to your fingers, it may be burning. But if you keep the leaf temperature cool by moving air and humidity, then the light can be brighter without doing harm.

Some orchids like all the direct sun they can get. If you have seen the vandaceous plants (arachnis, arandas, vandas and the like) growing in Southeast Asia in beds in the full sun, you know. Often their roots in the ground are covered with straw to keep them cooler.

Morning sun is more beneficial to plant growth than afternoon sun, as this is the active time of photosynthesis, the mysterious process by which plants form carbohydrates. Therefore, your greenhouse, or growing area, should be located in an area of maximum sunshine in the morning. The windowsill should face east or south.

Some orchids like more light than others, and some that require very bright sun won't flower in shade. Don't be afraid to put the sun-worshippers out in the sun. Just watch them for adverse reactions. Any changes should be gradual.

Growing orchids under lights is an important facet of this hobby, and many hobbyists are using artificial lights over plants that are grown in apartments, basements or bathrooms.

Ventilation

Remember this: orchids are air plants. Ventilation is important. They must have fresh air as they dislike stale, stuffy air. Fresh air keeps them supplied with carbon dioxide so necessary to their growth.

Ventilation is closely related to temperature.

Think of the breezes that blow around orchids growing in the treetops, and give your indoor plants as much ventilation as possible. But avoid cold drafts and sudden changes of temperature.

Even on a cold day, you can open one vent at the top of the greenhouse or crack a window in the plant room to make the air move. Hot air rises, so an opening at the opposite end from the heater will cause a slight air movement. In cold climates, don't open anything if it might get icy and not close. A fan running all the time will circulate air and eliminate stagnant pockets in a room

Oncidium macropetalum has dozens of one-inch yellow blooms on long sprays.

or a greenhouse. An old fashioned ceiling fan or a special greenhouse turbulator moves air if the greenhouse is high enough to suspend it from the ridge. A ceiling fan could be an attractive and useful addition to a plant room.

On warm days in humid climates, the greenhouse can be wide open and orchids will benefit from the fresh, moving air. In dry climates it might be better to keep the house closed and use an evaporative cooler to move the air and raise the humidity.

In places like South Florida and the Caribbean, where the trade winds blow, orchids growing outside may suffer from too much fresh air. The constant air movement may cause transpiration of moisture from leaves and bulbs faster than the roots can take it up. In such a situation, a windbreak helps.

Automatic greenhouse equipment keeps the environment congenial. Heater above, evaporative cooler below.

Orchids need air at their roots, too, and this cannot be overemphasized. This is why the potting mix is porous, why many orchids are grown in baskets, and why benches in orchid greenhouses are made of open material such as hardware cloth or pressed steel rather than a solid cover.

In cold climates greenhouses are built with low roofs to hold the heat and with steep roofs to unload the snow. In hot climates the greenhouses have high sides, and roofs raised as far as possible above the plants. This allows for air circulation and makes a cushion of moving air between the plants and the glass, which in turn moderates the heat.

Moving air in cold weather can prevent spotting of flowers in a humid atmosphere.

In climates where temperature and humidity are suitable, many growers put many plants outside during the warm months. They respond with vigorous growth. A chain securely attached between two trees is a good device for hanging plants outdoors. The filtered sunlight of the tree canopies may be just right for the orchids. Hooking the pot hangers into the chain links keeps them from sliding as they do on a wire or rope.

Humidity and Water

There is a distinct difference between the terms "humidity" and "watering."

WATERING means providing moisture at the roots by pouring it into the pot. Watering is one of the trickiest points of successful culture.

Orchids do not want to be constantly wet at the roots; rather, to be thoroughly watered and then allowed to dry out to some extent. Remember two rules. If in doubt, don't water. And when you water, do it thoroughly. Never give just a little. A plant either needs water or it doesn't. Fill pot to the rim, let it drain and flood it again.

How often to water depends upon the temperature, the humidity, the size and kind of pot, the type and density of the growing medium, the age and the stage of growth of the plant. Therefore, you need to group your plants according to type (genera), pot size, growth cycle and medium and water them accordingly.

You might water everything in your collection thoroughly once a week, the phalaenopsis and paphiopedilums at midweek and the seedlings every other day. Your conditions and watering schedules will change with the seasons and the number of cloudy days and other factors which affect evaporation.

When to water is something you have to learn by experience, and when you have mastered it, your thumb will turn green.

Remember that plants without pseudobulbs need watering more often than those with pseudobulbs.

Orchids in nature take a rest period during the dry season, and most of the species in cultivation observe a definite period when growth is slowed down. Some must be forced to rest to mature the growth and set flower buds, otherwise they will make more vegetative growth instead of flowers, and probably the growth will be weak and spindly.

Cutting down on water during rest does not mean to dehydrate the plants so that they shrivel. Nor does it mean to give less water. Water thoroughly, but do it less often.

One way to figure on whether or not a plant needs water is to poke your finger well down into the center of the medium and see if it is still damp.

Another way to do until you get the hang of it is to take a pot of the same size, fill it with the same potting medium, and set it on the bench next to one you are experimenting with. Water the same amount at the same time. Then when you are in doubt about watering again, empty the pot that has no plant in it, and see how much moisture remains in the medium.

All this is really not so hard, as you will learn by experience and be able to more or less play it by ear — or instinct — as your plants respond to your treatment.

Tap water as is comes from the hose is suitable in most areas, but if your orchids are not thriving, have the water analyzed. Too much sodium can be detrimental. Rain water is ideal, and orchids which can be grown outside benefit from showers, but in sections of typhoons or hurricanes, it may be necessary to move plants to shelter in times of excessive rains. This pertains to plants in containers. Obviously those naturalized on trees cannot be pulled off but their roots are exposed and dry out almost instantly.

In cold weather, take care that water is not cold enough to shock the roots. You may need to warm it to air temperature before applying.

A water breaker nozzle for your hose permits application of a great amount of water very quickly, which soaks the medium without washing it out of the pot or knocking over the small pots.

To water houseplants, carry them to the sink, run water through the pots thoroughly but gently, and let them stay in the sink for an hour to drain. Just pouring a little bit on top of the pot so it does not run out onto the table or plant stand does not provide water all through the pot.

Too much water may be worse than not enough. Watch your plants closely and try to anticipate their needs.

HUMIDITY refers to the moisture content of the air. Think about orchids in the wilds growing on rocks or trees near waterfalls, being drenched by early morning mists or fogs, then dried off by the midday sun and brisk breezes.

You can raise the humidity in your greenhouse or growing area by putting moisture into the air. If you have a mist nozzle on your hose you can mist the plants, benches and walkways to raise the humidity. This also lowers leaf temperature on hot days.

Evaporative cooling devices pull air into the greenhouse through wet pads. Mist sprinklers in the greenhouse can raise the humidity in a few minutes with automatic or manual controls.

Don't mist your plants overhead on dull days or when the air feels damp and chilly. Don't do this late in the day when water won't evaporate from foliage by nightfall. This invites rots and fungus diseases. Having the water applied in a fine mist cuts down on splashing fungus diseases from one plant to another, so the finer the droplets the better.

If you live where days are frequently dull, such overhead misting may do harm. But if you have sunlight and moving air, the plants love it. And you may even want to mist certain plants late in the day, contrary to the general statement above, if it is going to be a hot night. Misting then would cool the foliage and refresh the plants, just like getting under a shower would make you feel better.

Getting the humidity up to an acceptable level for orchids is the hardest phase of growing them in your home.

A plastic quart bottle with a mist sprayer nozzle to work by hand is good for misting foliage but does not raise the humidity content of the air very much.

Fertilizer

Fertilizing of orchids is a variable practice. Growers who pot in fir bark must fertilize, usually with a 30-10-10 formula for the simple reason that the bark does not contain enough nitrogen for plant growth, and without nitrogen plants cannot survive. Further, the wood-rotting fungus which breaks down the bark is voracious in its consumption of nitrogen, and unless you supply it, the fungus will steal from the orchid plant. The 30-10-10 formula represents 30 parts nitrogen, 10 parts each of phosphorous and potassium, the three major elements in plant fertilizers. The surplus of nitrogen supplies the fungus with about 20 percent, the orchid plant gets about 10 percent.

Other formulas used with bark are 21-7-14 or 30-10-20 and the like.

Orchids in other materials benefit from fertilizer but the nitrogen need not be as heavy. A balanced formula such as 10-10-10 or 18-18-18 is suitable for most mediums. However, where light is bright and air is moving, fish emulsion, 5-1-1, works well with tree fern. Many hobby growers prefer to alternate feedings of one brand and one formula with others. There are special orchid fertilizers with definite recommendations for use on certain plants.

There is a relationship between the growth cycle and the environmental factors and the amount of fertilizer a plant can use.

Stanhopea candida must be grown in a hanging basket because it blooms from the bottom of the plant.

In climates where winter days are overcast more often than not, the fertilizer must be considerably reduced to compensate for the lack of sunlight.

In potting materials other than bark, fertilizing is suggested all during the period of active growth, with either less or none for plants that take a definite period of rest. Orchids without pseudobulbs, including paphiopedilums, phalaenopsis, and the vandaceous group, generally need fertilizer year round, with the amount or the frequency decreased in dull weather. Cymbidium growers frequently switch to a low nitrogen such as 2-10-10 after vegetative growths are made up.

In bark, many growers fertilize with almost every watering. However, it is possible to build up a concentration of harmful fertilizer salts in the pot, and so it is necessary to use clear water and flush the pot thoroughly every three or four applications.

It is important to give frequent light feedings rather than heavy, infrequent feedings. When you do fertilize, pour it on so all the roots are saturated.

There are a great many orchid fertilizers on the market, and you must mix and apply each exactly according to directions. Then watch your plants and time your frequency and dilution according to their reactions. Every grower has his favorite fertilizer. Orchid growers in Ceylon recommend elephant dung.

All plants need certain trace elements in addition to the three major fertilizer elements. Some of these are available in the potting material, some may be in the water. If any are missing, plants may suffer. Most fertilizers include the minor elements in minute quantities, and so this is rarely a problem.

Plants can absorb nutrients through their foliage, so the fertilizer

Epidendrum pseudepidendrum is a cane orchid with startling orange and green flowers.

that gets on the leaves while being applied to the pot is beneficial.

There are any number of gadgets for applying fertilizer with the hose, mixing it with water as applied. Just follow directions so the quantity is as specified on the package, or lighter.

If you are trying a new brand, take it easy and watch for response from the plants. Don't think that twice as much is better. Too much fertilizer burns roots and stunts growth.

Never fertilize a dry plant. Water it thoroughly first.

Correlation is the Key

All of these factors of good growth — light, air, temperature moisture, fertilizer, are so closely related that your main effort must be to work out a balance.

Plants grown in bright light can use more fertilizer and water and moving air than plants grown in dim light. This is because sunlight is the energy which runs the chemical process which converts the various elements into plant food and then new growth. When the sun is bright, the process is more productive if the raw materials are there for the plant to work with.

On the other hand, plants in too much light shut down their manufacturing processes, as water which they need for the process evaporates too rapidly from the leaf surface.

Temperature affects the rate of growth, and a plant in a congenial temperature range can function, whereas one that is too hot or too cold cannot use any fertilizer or take up much water because it is not active.

Water needs to be supplied in a ratio comparable to the rate the plant can use it, and sufficiently to offset moisture lost into the air. High humidity reduces this moisture loss, leaving more water within the plant for use in growth processes.

It all sounds very complicated, but it isn't, really As you work with your plants you will sense any environmental factors that are out of balance, and when everything is in harmony, your plants will thrive.

Doritaenopsis Asahi 'McQuerry' AM/AOS. Doritaenopsis crosses increase the size of the Doritis parent and often bloom in the summer.

CHAPTER III

POTTING

Potting of orchids is a most controversial subject. Every grower has his favorite potting medium, definite choice of pot type, and ideas about when and how to repot.

Time was when nearly everybody in the United States potted in osmunda. The Hawaiians shifted to tree fern (hapuu), the West Coast people almost unanimously went into fir bark.

Now there are people dedicated to osmunda, tree fern, bark or rock; some who use mixtures, and some who jump into every new medium that comes along.

In other countries growers use asplenium fiber, coconut husks, burnt earth, volcanic cinders and other items.

Each new material that comes along stirs up a lot of interest, and is ballyhooed as curing all ills. So let me caution you.

If your plants are growing and flowering well in what you are now using, stick with it for the majority. When something new interests you, try it on a few plants. Don't shift your whole collection at once into something you know little about.

Plants have to get accustomed to a new medium. But so do you. You must learn to pot with it, to water it, to fertilize it.

But, since new things will come along constantly, don't be afraid to experiment. Just prove your ability to manage a new mix before repotting many of your plants. Take plants through a second growth and flowering.

If you use more than one potting mixture, keep together the plants that are in each kind. And you will use more than one thing, because you know that cymbidiums and paphiopedilums need a special compost, basket plants need a medium that drains quickly, and some orchids do well on slabs.

When and How to Repot

Since almost all of these potting materials break down in time, and since sympodial plants move forward and walk right over the side of the pot, repotting of sympodial plants is necessary every year or two. Monopodial plants may go forever without a shift, such as strapleaf vandas once they are of mature size and in a large basket. The roots will be mainly in the air and not in the container anyhow. Refill the basket occasionally.

A general rule is to repot a sympodial plant when new roots are visible at the base of a bulb. Clean off the old mixture and pot with the back end of the plant near the rim of the pot so the plant can move forward.

Choose a pot of a size that will accommodate two new bulbs, generally about one-third larger than the old pot unless you divide the plant into smaller divisions or take off the back bulbs.

While you have the plant out of the pot, take off all the old potting mixture. Go over the plant carefully for pests, especially mites or scale insects under the leaves. Pull off brown growth sheaths. Cut off old flower spikes. Clip off dead roots and damaged leaves, using sterilized tools. Dust cut surfaces with fungicide, even where you cut through the rhizome to divide a plant.

Always use clean pots, and even wash new pots before using. Scrub used pots in hot water and detergent with a stiff brush, soak in a solution of one part Clorox to 10 parts water for 30 minutes. Then rinse thoroughly and drain. Clean up your stakes, pot hangers, drainage cocks at the same time lest they transmit disease to another plant.

Put drainage material into the pot first. Use crocks (broken pots), charcoal, pebbles, or tree fern chunks. Hold the plant in position and work the potting medium around and under it. With bark or tree fern, pour it around and firm with a blunt instrument. Watch those eyes or new leads and don't break them off. It is easy to do.

Stake and tie the plant so it doesn't jiggle or fall out of the pot, Use a pot clip from the rim across the rhizome or over the roots.

When repotting replace labels that are becoming illegible, damaged or brittle because a plant without a name is an orphan. Tie labels securely to pot clips or stakes, or around the bulbs. Multicolored plastic wires from telephone cables are excellent for tying up plants and attaching labels.

For pictures of the repotting procedure see "You Can Grow Cattleya Orchids."

Potting Mediums

With any potting medium the choice of particle size, if it comes in a variety of shapes and sizes, depends on the size of the plant roots.

For instance, mature vandas with roots as big as pencils, require a very open medium of chunky material so air is available between the material. Cattleyas and phalaenopsis have roots of medium thickness, can use a medium grade to provide air spaces. Whereas orchids with fine roots, such as miltonias, lycastes, some oncidiums, and many seedlings, do better in a finer medium. Their roots are small in circumference, can move easily through a fine medium and find enough air spaces yet snuggle comfortably into the potting material.

TREE FERN (HAPUU). Tree fern fiber harvested from trunks of tree ferns in Hawaii, Mexico and other tropical areas, makes good potting material for orchids.

It may be bought in shreds of fine, medium or coarse grade; small or large chunks; slabs, logs, baskets or totem poles; even figures shaped like monkeys.

Tree fern is easy to pot with. Small chunks may serve as drainage material in the bottom of pots where another grade is used around the roots.

Baskets carved of tree fern are excellent for large hanging plants such as vandas and angraecums. Roots penetrate right through the fiber, and plants seldom need repotting. Slabs are excellent for plants that like to run, such as bulbophyllums. Tie plants on with plastic wire, securely so they don't wobble, or fasten with hairpins. Put a little sphagnum moss over the roots to help retain moisture until they penetrate the fiber of the slab.

Generally speaking, tree fern requires more frequent watering than osmunda, but less often than bark. Plants on slabs dry out quickly and may need special attention unless it is their nature to be dry.

OSMUNDA — This is the root of the cinnamon fern. It is coarse and fibrous, and may be black and wiry or light brown and softer. It is scarce and expensive. It is dug from swamps and should be washed free of soil before use.

Osmunda needs to be packed around the roots into the container so tightly that the plant stands upright and does not wobble. This takes a strong arm. It is done by pushing chunks into the pot at the rim while holding the plant in position.

Osmunda holds water longer than most potting mediums, therefore does not require watering as frequently. It is very important that plants in large pots dry out in the middle before the next watering, as the osmunda may be soggy below the surface while appearing to be dry.

FIR BARK — Bark from white fir trees, red fir trees and Douglas fir, this last not a true fir, is a very popular potting medium for orchids.

Bark comes generally in three sizes, fine, medium and coarse, depending on the length of the particles. All fines and dust should be removed before use.

Bark needs to be soaked in water for a few hours prior to use, as it is difficult to get it wet. In fact, it is difficult to keep it too wet, which makes bark a good medium for beginners since it can't be easily overwatered.

Dendrobium aggregatum hanging in a tree fern basket has flowers like showers of gold coins.

On the other hand, it dries out so rapidly that careful attention is needed to keep plants moist during periods of warm weather and low humidity.

Orchids in bark must be fertilized with a high nitrogen formula. See section on Fertilizer.

MIXTURES — There are as many potting mixes as there are growers using them. Formulas containing bark, coarse peat, redwood bark or redwood fiber are popular. Perlite, turkey grit, decayed oak leaves, sedge peat and other substances may be included.

ROCK — Various types of rock are used for growing orchids, and trade names differ. Rock has the advantage of not disintegrating, as all the other media will do in time, but here again, anybody using it must learn how to handle it. Plants in rock and those in other mediums cannot be grown with the same culture, in all probability.

TERRESTRIAL ORCHIDS — Phaius, calanthes, and other terrestrials require potting mix that may include soil, dehydrated dairy manure, humus and other elements used for house and garden plants. Semi-terrestrials, such as paphiopedilums and cymbidiums require their own special mixes.

Containers

CLAY POTS — Clay pots have been the standard containers for more than a century. They come in many sizes. Some growers prefer those with slit slides, some like the shallower types called azalea pots or bulb pans for phalaenopsis, community pots and seedlings. Roots are a few degrees cooler in clay pots than in plastic.

Clay pots are porous, permit evaporation through the sides of the pots as well as from the top of the medium.

PLASTIC POTS — The people who favor plastic pots think they are the greatest. They are not porous, cut watering chores to half the frequency and do not accumulate fertilizer salts on their sides.

Small seedlings grown in quantities do well in square plastic pots placed rim to rim, as there is no air moving about them to dry out the compost, and watering is needed less often.

Some cut flower growers get splendid production from meristem cattleyas grown in large white plastic pots up to 14-inch size, the plants potted in a water-retentive bark and peat formula that is a modification of the original Off mix.

Just like the mediums, the choice of pots depends on what works best for you. The controversy between the clay pot growers and the plastic pot people is spirited. But the fact remains that plants do better for some people if grown in plastic, and for other people in clay.

BASKETS — Baskets for hanging plants should be of cypress

or redwood, with the bottom slats fairly close together to hold the medium in place.

You can buy decorative hanging containers for your family room or porch, set potted plants inside when in bloom, and put them on display, changing plants as flowers fade.

Baskets made of tree fern are useful. If a plant outgrows one size, merely insert basket and all (the fiber will be full of roots) into a larger size.

Take care to water basket plants thoroughly, and to keep the humidity high. Naturally, hanging plants with such open containers will dry out fast. Most of them have many roots outside the basket anyhow.

TUBS — Wooden boxes or tubs are fine containers for large cymbidiums. They should be constructed with the bottoms raised slightly above the base of the sides so drainage holes don't clog up. Only the most durable woods should be used.

SLABS AND LOGS — In nature, epiphytic orchids grow on tree limbs, in rock crevices, and sometimes on decaying wood if their host tree fell to the ground or a branch broke off, taking the orchids with it.

You can make attractive hanging containers from pieces of hardwood with rough bark, but these rot in time. A better choice is a log or slab of tree fern or of cork bark.

You can attach plants with hairpins or wire florist staples, tie them on with wire or string, and work a bit of sphagnum moss around the roots if you wish. Rattail oncidiums such as Onc. jonesianum, which like to be relatively dry, grow beautifully on hanging slabs of cork bark.

Large slabs may be used for a colony of plants of one kind, which make a good show when in bloom and, of course, grow compatibly together.

UNCONVENTIONAL CONTAINERS — Phalaenopsis look lovely in a strawberry jar (See "You Can Grow Phalaenopsis Orchids.") Other containers may be used for orchids providing they have sufficient drainage. If you experiment, watch plants carefully and make adjustments necessary to keep them happy.

Orchid collecting is great fun either by caravan on land or by boat on the Amazon. Left, a tree of epiphytes. Opposite page, orchid country in Bolivia.

Some of the people on these pages are Fred and Barbara Fuchs, Jack McQuerry, Fran Gay and Fred B. Noble. For the orchids we found see pages 27, 37, 43, 56 and 92.

Oncidium stacyi, a new species from Bolivia with terete leaves a yard long.

CHAPTER IV

THE ORCHIDS

Which orchids should you grow?

Will you be a specialist, growing only cymbidiums or cattleyas or vandas, depending on your geographic location?

Or will you be a collector of several types? Most small collections are mixtures, and this makes for variety in flower types, sizes and colors, blooming seasons and cultural practices.

Many different types of orchids will grow well together in the same environment, providing you give them the diversified attention they need. Not all types are compatible, and you must choose according to minimum and maximum temperatures, light intensity and other factors.

The orchid growers publish fascinating advertisements and catalogs to tempt you.

Don't begin with awarded, expensive plants. You must practice and learn to grow orchids, so choose less expensive plants to begin with. We all kill a few along the way. But always buy healthy, vigorous plants. Sickly plants are no bargain at any price.

Shop around. Visit the nurseries nearest you. Write for the catalogs. Study the ads. Visit other amateurs. Go to the shows. And choose the orchids that you like the best . . . and that grow well for you.

Cattleya

(Abbreviation C.)

Hybridizing of Cattleyas within the genus and with other related genera has produced a fascinating and fabulous array of flowers in many sizes and colors.

Cattleyas are the most familiar orchids, and purple comes first to mind. There are 60 or more species of the genus Cattleya native to Central America and South America, some of which are large and purple, others are white, yellow, green, bronze and assorted colors.

LABIATE CATTLEYAS — This group includes the species with single leaves atop the pseudobulbs and large, showy flowers. Such familiar species as Cattleya mossiae, Cattleya trianaei and the yellow Cattleya dowiana belong in this group. Hybrids of these species into successive generations have given us today's large hybrids which are near perfection in color, form and size.

The alba or white forms of the labiate species are the ancestors of the many large fine white cattleyas now available. C. Bow Bells, registered in 1945, set a standard of excellence in succeeding generations.

BIFOLIATE CATTLEYAS — The species with two or three leaves at the top of a pseudobulb have flowers generally of smaller size, sometimes heavier substance, and interesting colors. Some have spots. Some produce clusters of many flowers.

Cattleya guttata, Cattleya aurantiaca, Cattleya aclandiae and Cattleya granulosa, among others, have produced some very exotic orchids in yellows, greens, bronzes and other art shades.

The genus is named for William Cattley. Pronounce it "CAT-lee-uh."

LAELIOCATTLEYA (Abbreviation Lc.) — Laelias are closely related to cattleyas, generally having smaller flowers but some species are brightly colored. Laelia tenebrosa, Laelia flava, Laelia purpurata are among species hybridized with cattleyas to intensify colors.

Pronunciation: "LAY-lee-uh," "LAY-lee-o-CAT-lee-uh."

Cattleya warscewiczii, a species (above); Potinara Eva Aspen, a multi-generic hybrid (below).

Cattleya Portia, a medium size cluster bifoliate hybrid.

BRASSOCATTLEYA (Bc.) — Brassavola digbyana is generally the ancestor in a large-flowered cattleya-type hybrid because it contributes the fringe on the lip. Brassavola nodosa, a small, white and green flower on a plant with pencil-like leaves, is very fragrant at night. Some interesting small-flowered hybrids have been made with this species and with B. glauca.

Pronunciation: "BRASS-o-CAT-lee-uh," "Bra-SAH-voh-la."

BRASSOLAELIOCATTLEYA (Blc.) — Get all three genera into the background and you have a trigeneric hybrid with a long name which should have large size, strong color and a fringed lip.

SOPHROCATTLEYA, SOPHROLAELIOCATTLEYA (Sc., Slc.) — Sophronitis grandiflora is a little three-inch flower of brilliant vermilion which intensifies the color of larger flowers in multigeneric crosses. Slc. Anzac 'Orchidhurst' FCC/RHS is a famous hybrid parent which has produced many additional colorful hybrids in orange and reddish-lavender shades, called art shades. "Sof-roh-NYE-tiss" is the pronunciation of the natural genus name.

OTHER HYBRIDS — Cattleyas cross readily with several other genera and many of these are interesting, including Cattleytonia (Cattleya x Broughtonia), Diacattleya (Diacrium x Cattleya), and Epicattleya (Epidendrum x Cattleya), to mention a few. All these related genera will cross with each other giving such hybrids as Brassotonia (Brassovola x Broughtonia) and Schombolaelia (Schomburgkia x Laelia). In more complicated combinations there are names which may honor a person such as Yamadara (Brassavola x Laelia x Cattleya x Epidendrum) and Vaughnara (Cattleya x Brassavola x Epidendrum).

CULTURE — A minimum of 55°F. at night is recommended for hybrids and species in this group. They can endure lower temperatures for a short period, but flowers or buds may suffer. With sunlight or artificial heat, the day temepratures may be 10 to 30 degrees higher.

In summer, the daytime maximum should be about 85°F. with a drop at night. Higher natural temperature can be endured if the

Laeliocattleya William of Woodlawn, a bifoliate hybrid with silky texture.

air is humid and moving so leaf surfaces stay cool and do not burn. Strong sunlight is possible with humidity and air circulation. However, cattleyas grown in strong light and warm temperatures need more water and fertilizer and humidity than those in shadier conditions and lower temperatures. The balance of factors is most important.

Cattleyas are grown in many different mediums and should be watered and fertilized accordingly. In cold climates where winter days are dull, it is very important that the potting mix dry out before water is given again.

The species have definite cycles of growth with noticeable resting periods which should be observed with less frequent watering and less fertilizer. Hybrids may be in active growth almost all the time and should be encouraged.

If a plant needs repotting, do it when new roots appear at the base of the bulb. See Potting.

Seedlings are grown just like mature plants except they need less light and the smaller pots generally need watering more often than larger pots. A good way to add to your collection is to buy seedlings that are nearly mature enough to bloom (about four-inch pot size). You may get some good flowers this way. Don't judge them on first bloom, as some improve with age.

For more information on these orchids see sequel book "You Can Grow Cattleya Orchids."

Cymbidium

(Abbreviation Cym.)

A greenhouse full of cymbidium blooms is dazzling. There are many colors, including the pastels. The greens are vivid, the pinks lovely, the yellows brilliant and the odd shades fascinating.

The number of flowers and the durability of the blooms add to the attractiveness of these orchids.

Cymbidiums have been developed to a high degree of perfection.

Phalaenopsis equestris 'Mary Noble' CCM/AOS received a Certificate of Cultural Merit when it produced 151 flowers plus 150 buds. The flowers are less than an inch wide, light pink with lavender lips.

The finest flowers are round, clear and sparkling. New hybrids are coming on the market all the time, and by studying the awarded plants at shows you can learn to distinguish outstanding flowers from those that are average.

Unlike cattleyas, cymbidiums have been hybridized with only two other genera, so you are dealing only with plants of one genus developed through many generations from a few species.

The great majority of cymbidiums come into bloom in the spring, providing florist flowers for Easter and Mother's Day. While in a large collection the season may extend through almost half a year, helped by the durability of the flowers and the number of blooms per spike, spring is the season. Sprays may last a month when cut, individual blooms on the plants may endure much longer. Flowers should be fully open for about 10 days prior to being cut.

Today's fine hybrid cymbidiums are descended from species that are native to the Himalayan regions of Asia, where the climate is characterized by heavy rainfall and cool nights. These factors must be remembered if cymbidiums in cultivation are to be grown successfully.

Miniature cymbidiums have been developed using small species native to Japan, China and Australia with standard sizes. The flowers are attractive, though smaller, but the plants are smaller, too. They are somewhat easier to bloom indoors than the regular size cymbidiums.

POTTING MIXTURES — Every cymbidium grower has his own favorite mixture and his preference for containers. Some use plastic pots, others clay pots, wooden tubs or ground beds.

Cymbidiums are terrestrial plants, but the soil mixture must be able to retain moisture while at the same time draining enough so it is not soaking wet.

Here are some suggested mixtures:

8 parts fir bark (¼ to ⅝" size)
2 parts dry oak leaves

Center: Cattleya warscewiczii. Clockwise from top left: Schomburgkia undulata, Epidendrum atropurpureum var. randii, Oncidium lanceanum, Aganisia cyanea, Trichopilia suavis, Pescatorea lehmanni, Miltonia vexallaria, Sobralia rosea, Phragmipedium longifolium.

Another:

  2 parts fir bark
  2 parts coarse oak leaves
  1 part fine sand
  2 parts German or Canadian peat
  3 parts redwood fiber

And to every 2 cu. feet of this mixture add 1 handful hoof and horn meal, 12 oz. dolomite lime, 1 to 2 oz. superphosphate.

Still another typical mixture:

  2 parts redwood bark, fir bark or wood shavings
  1 part peat or oak leaves

Grind together, add 10% sand (optional), plus a little superphosphate and agricultural lime.

Another mix for beds: equal parts redwood fiber, coarse poultry peat, fir bark, plus ½ part perlite, plus small amounts of ground limestone, raw bonemeal, nitrogen and superphosphate, at the rate of about one eight-inch pot of limestone and one three-inch pot each of the others to a wheelbarrow of the mixture. This mix should stand a few weeks before planting.

It is important, whatever the combination, that the mixture be high in organic matter, that it drain readily and that the pH be about 6.0. Some growers offer packaged cymbidium mix and this is the easiest solution.

Plants are best divided in the spring right after flowering, at which time the leafless back bulbs should be removed. If the potting mix is still in good condition, you can shift the plants without dividing or shaking off the old mixture, but if soil has deteriorated, shake it off and push new material around the roots. Allow pot size sufficient for two or three years' growth, as they dislike being disturbed.

CULTURE — Temperature seems to be a critical factor in inducing cymbidiums to set buds, it being necessary to have a decided drop in temperature at night in late summer and early fall to initiate the buds.

In warm climates, this can be achieved by the use of cooling equipment.

During growth, daytime temperature can go to 90°F. but a range of 75-80° is better. There must be moving air. In a controlled greenhouse the night temperature should be around 50°, but this is not always possible with amateur growers. At any rate, the nights should be decidedly cooler than the days, and at time of bud initiation (August and September) by 20° to 30°.

In winter, plants can stand almost freezing without damage, but flower spike damage may occur. However, if night temperature during winter is over 60°F. the buds may drop.

Cymbidiums should never be dried out, so the pots should be watered at once when the top of the potting material begins to look dry. During the summer, cymbidiums need lots of water, but the drainage needs to be adequate so water does not stand. Even in the dull, cool days of winter the compost should never get dry, although less water will be needed.

If you use more than one type of container, you will have to check each plant individually to determine when it needs water.

Overhead mist spraying with a fine nozzle benefits plants on summer days as it raises the humidity and reduces the evaporation.

Cymbidiums need as much light as you can give them without burning the leaves. In the Northeast and in the Pacific Northwest, you can put plants out in full sun in the summer if there is moving air. In hot climates you need to supply sufficient light, at the same time keeping the temperature within a desirable range.

During the growing season the light can range from 4,000 to 7,000-foot candles, depending on temperature, humidity and ventilation. During the flowering season, shade is intensified to preserve the colors, especially of green and yellow flowers.

Cymbidiums which are grown with ample light and moisture can use frequent applications of fertilizer. Here again, the formulas and practices are as numerous as the growers.

Liquid fertilizers may be applied every week to 10 days. The formula might be 30-10-10 from January through July, with a low-nitrogen such as 6-30-30 the other five months. Whatever you use, dilute and apply as specified by the manufacturer, and remember that plants must have light in order to use fertilizer for growth.

Top to bottom: Doritaenopsis Corcata, Phalaenopsis Jack McQuerry, Dendrobium phalaenopsis hybrid.

Top to bottom: Cattleya guttata alba; Meristems of Laeliocattleya S.J. Bracey 'Wailani' AM/AOS and Brassolaeliocattleya Norman's Bay 'Low' FCC/RHS.

SEEDLINGS — Seedlings can be grown with higher night temperatures all year long because you are interested in maximum growth and not in setting flower spikes. Higher humidity and somewhat lower light intensity than for adult plants are recommended for seedlings.

Phalaenopsis
(Abbreviation Phal.)

Phalaenopsis are easy to grow where there is sufficient warmth, and because they can grow in subdued light, are amenable houseplants. Because they are medium size or small plants, they take less space than many other orchids and so are suitable for limited windowsills or artificial light growing arrangements. The reward in flowers is great, as many of them produce long sprays of durable blooms.

White phalaenopsis are the brides' orchids, being unsurpassed as wedding flowers.

And while the whites are the most famous of the genus, there are intriguing phalaenopsis in a vivid array of colors, with new ones coming along every day.

Large pinks and small pinks make showers of flowers in the greenhouse, and some of the new hybrids hold up extremely well as cut flowers.

One line of breeding brings in white flowers with red or rosy lips. These are lovely.

Phalaenopsis of star shape descended from Phalaenopsis lueddemanniana, have become popular, and many hybrids of this type are being introduced.

Yellow phalaenopsis have been combined with other colors to give interesting variations.

Novelty phalaenopsis are those using some of the lesser known species of odd coloring to produce flowers of bronze, moss rose, lavender and other off shades. Flowers with spots, stripes and irregular markings are interesing.

Pronunciation: "FAIL-en-OP-sis."

CULTURE — Phalaenopsis come from warm areas of Southeast Asia and plants like to be warm all year. While they grow best at a range between 65° and 85°F. summer temperatures can be higher if humidity is high and shade is sufficient. And while night temperature should not go much below this minimum, a drop in temperature to 55 degrees at night for three or four weeks in fall or winter initiates flower spikes.

Phalaenopsis generally flower in the late winter and spring, having set their buds and started their spikes in the fall. On the West Coast, where nights are cool all year, phalaenopsis set more second, third or even fourth spikes than here in the Southeast where nights are warmer.

In a greenhouse with coolers the phals bloom intermittently all year with the biggest display in the spring.

Many phalaenopsis can be persuaded to make secondary spikes after flowers are cut if the lower part of the old stem remains.

Phalaenopsis grow in any of the standard potting materials. In our collection they do well in tree fern chunks.

Phalaenopsis like to be constantly moist, and it is important that the medium drains because watering is frequent. Water should be warmed in winter if it is cooler than the air temperature. And watering should be done early in the day so the foliage is dry by night. Crown rot is generally caused by water standing in the crown during low temperatures.

Phalaenopsis make large plants with succulent leaves, and their vigorous root systems search out nutrients. Any fertilizer used for other orchids is suitable, and if potted in bark, a high nitrogen formula is necessary. Feeding can be frequent during periods of warm weather and active growth.

Phalaenopsis need less light than many other orchids because their big leaves burn easily. A range between 1,000 and 1,800-foot-candles is suitable. Some growers give more light and use humidi-

Top to bottom: Vandachnis Premier, Vanda Rothschildiana, Ascocenda Yip Sum Wah.

Top left: Phaius tankervilliae;
Top right: Paphiopedilum Edward Marshall Boehm;
Lower right: Paphiopedilum concolor;
Lower left: "Jewel orchid," Ludisia discolor.

fiers and fans to keep plants from burning. If plants have more light, they need more water and can use more fertilizer.

Seedlings should be grown in more shade, and any recently potted plants or sickly plants without roots should be shaded until growth is evident.

Air movement is important to the good health of phalaenopsis, but it must be warm, moist air. Cold drafts harm the plants and cause the buds to drop.

Slight air movement is important where flowers are open to prevent spotting. Use a fan, crack a vent or open a window at a distance from the heat source to move the air.

DORITAENOPSIS (Dtps.) — Phalaenopsis crossed with Doritis pulcherrima make hybrids with the best of both parents. Now several generations from the species, the doritaenopsis hybrids have flowers in a wide color range, size equal to straight phalaenopsis in some crosses, and often the heavier substance of the small parent.

Dtps. Red Coral (Dor. pulcherrima x Phal. Doris) is a popular parent with colorful progeny.

MULTIGENERIC HYBRIDS — Phalaenopsis have been crossed with a dozen or more other genera in bigeneric and multigeneric combination. Use of the vandaceous group brings in vivid colors with renantheras, rhynchostylis and ascocentrums. At present writing there are more than three dozen multigenerics in this group.

Much more information on all aspects of phalaenopsis culture and breeding is in the sequel book in this series, "You Can Grow Phalaenopsis."

Vanda

(Abbreviation V.)

Vandas are warm climate orchids. They love the sun and the rain and the tropical breezes.

These are orchids of exciting colors — yellow and brown, pink and green, apricot, cerise, amethyst, blue and violet.

Vandas are monopodial orchids, and produce their flowers in upright spikes of several blooms. Many plants will have two or more spikes in bloom at once and some bloom almost constantly.

Vandas can be divided into groups.

TERETE VANDAS — Terete (pronounced "TEAR-eat") means "circular" or "cyndrical," and you can instantly recognize a terete vanda because the stems and leaves are round like pencils.

The most famous of this group is Vanda Miss Joaquim, the little lavender flower that is grown by the acre and sold by the pound for leis or souvenirs in Hawaii, and grown as hedges in so many gardens in Singapore where it originated.

Vanda teres, V. hookeriana and their variations including alba forms are teretes.

STRAPLEAF VANDAS — The term strapleaf describes the vandas in this category, which have foliage like ribbons or straps. These have been hybridized through several generations. The most famous parent is Vanda sanderana (correctly Euanthe sanderana), a spectacular species from the Philippines which imparts color, size and form to its hybrids. Also important is V. coerulea, the blue-flowered species, which is used for color. V. Rothschildiana, a hybrid of these two species, is famous for its size, floriferousness and the lavender-blue color of its round, flat blooms.

SEMI-TERETE VANDAS — A third classification concerns those hybrids between terete and strapleaf vandas, which have gone into several generations with interesting results.

These plants have somewhat wider leaves than the teretes, but more rounded and fleshy than the strapleaf types. Leaves are indented with narrow grooves.

ASCOCENDA (Ascda.) — Called 'miniature vandas," the hybrids of the large vandas with diminutive, closely related orchids, ascocentrums, are extremely popular. The ascocentrums hold down the plant size and add to the color. In succeeding generations of breeding some of the flowers are almost as large as strapleaf vanda hybrids, but the favored ones are somewhat smaller. Ascocentrum curvifolium is the species most used as a parent. Pronunciation "ass-ko-SEN-trum."

Top to bottom: "Leopard orchid," Ansellia gigantea; Bulbophyllum vaginatum, Aeranthes grandiflora.

Cymbidium finlaysonianum (pendant); Cymbidium Mimi (miniature); Cymbidium Mauritius (standard).

The ascocenda blooms are round and flat and brightly colored like strapleaf vandas, produced on upright spikes at frequent intervals, and last a long time. Yet the plants are a fraction the size of mature strapleaf vandas, and where space is a problem, several ascocendas can be accommodated where only one mature vanda would fit.

Ascocenda plants in bloom provide delightful coffee table decoration or fillers for hanging containers indoors or on a patio. Individual blooms of the smaller-flowering types are fine for boutonnieres.

CULTURE — Vandas originate in the warm climates of Southeast Asia with the exception of the blue Vanda coerulea and others which grow in the cool, high altitude areas in the Himalayas.

The species may bloom at set seasons, but well-grown hybrids may flower several times a year.

Vandas like sunlight, the teretes more than the strapleaves. Teretes are grown outdoors in the brightest sunlight in warm climates. Strapleaf vandas do well outdoors in semi-shade in warm weather, grow under glass or plastic in colder weather. Vandas are not suitable for houseplants unless light is much brighter than in the ordinary home.

Along with bright sun, vandas require copious watering and immediate drainage. They can be misted on sunny days one or more times.

Moving air is important, too, as this helps to lower leaf temperature of the strapleaves when the sun is bright and hot. Leaves burn quickly, especially at the change of the seasons, yet in a greenhouse vandas need to hang near the glass for maximum light. Even the semi-teretes, if grown outdoors, should not be suddenly shifted so their shady side is toward the light or the sun will burn them.

Vandas grow in any potting medium so long as it is porous. Large pots, baskets or slabs are suitable containers. Teretes and semi-teretes can be fastened with plant ties to tree fern posts and will put some of their roots into the fiber.

Fertilizing needs to be in tune with the bright light, porous medium and frequent flowering of these plants. Since so many of the roots hang outside the containers, foliar feeding (and aerial root feeding) supplement fertilizer applied to the potting mixtures. During warm weather, once a week is not too often to spray vandas with a dilute fertilizer solution.

Vandas are very durable plants, and while they prefer to be on the warm side of the thermometer, plants can survive brief periods of very cold weather. However, bud spikes may be stunted or fail to develop. Daytime temperatures can go into the 80's or 90's providing there is moving air and high humidity.

Other Vandaceous Orchids

Several other genera of orchids related to the Vandas are of interest, especially in warm climates.

ARACHNIS (Arach.) — The bizarre spider orchids of the genus Arachnis need strong sunlight and grow to great heights; 10-foot plants are not unusual.

AERIDES (Aer.) — These monopodials are smaller in stature than the rampant plants of related genera, have pendant or arching inflorescences of mainly white and rose purple blooms, usually very fragrant.

RENANTHERA (Ren.) — Renantheras are long-legged plants with spikes of brilliant colored reddish-orange blooms with open shape. Renantheras must have bright sun.

RHYNCHOSTYLIS (Rhy.) — Foxtail orchids with pendant or upright spikes of small flowers, closely placed together. Very attractive. Plants best grown in hanging baskets but are much shorter in height than other mature vandaceous plants. Rhy. gigantea has brilliant magenta blooms, also forms that are pure white or white with amethyst spots.

MULTIGENERICS — All of the above, plus other vandaceous orchids, have been crossed to make colorful and floriferous hybrids. Generic names include Renancentrum, Renanopsis, Renantanda, Rhynchovanda, Aeridovanda, even Nobleara, named for this author, which is Aerides x Vanda x Renanthera.

1972 Marion R. Sheehan

If you have sufficient light and space, you will find the vandaceous orchids very rewarding for they are easy to grow and generous with flowers.

Paphiopedilum

(Paph.)

The tropical slipper orchids from Asia are very exotic. They are small plants which don't take up much space and are attractive even when not in flower. The blooms, which are very long lasting (several weeks under normal conditions), come in interesting colors, artistic patterns and combinations.

For years writers have written that the mottled leaved types were "warm growing," and the plain green-leaved types were "cool growing" and they could not grow well together. People also said paphs would not grow in warm climates. That they liked coolness and shade. In our experience, none of this is true.

We grow, here in Jacksonville, Florida, paphs with plain and mottled leaves side by side on the bench. We grow all of them in very bright light, generally 2,000 foot candles or more at mid-day, and temperatures of 80°F. or more at midday.

Clockwise from top left: Epidendrum ibaguense, Peristeria elata, Neomoorea irrorata, Masdevallia coccinea, Telipogon hemimelas, Anguloa rueckeri, Masdevallia chimaera, Anguloa clowesii.

Paphiopedilum Enhanced, a lime and lemon slipper (Golden Acres x Gwenpur).

But, we keep the air moving with a turbulator, we run coolers in the summer, we open the roof vent and the doors on balmy winter days, and we run overhead mist sprinklers to keep the humidity up. The paphs do beautifully! And they grow in the same 15x32-foot greenhouse with phalaenopsis, cattleyas, vandas, agraecums, oncidiums, and many other genera.

Our mix for paphs is Canadian peat moss, perlite, river gravel, shredded sphagnum moss, with additions of superphosphate, cow manure and bonemeal, wet thoroughly before potting the plants in clay pots.

We water and fertilize our paphs along with everything else,

We grow paphs in Florida with bright sunlight, high humidity and moving air. Mottled leaf and plain leaf types grow side by side. Some seedlings are under the bench.

generally every weekend, sometimes we water again at midweek but not always. Our fertilizer solution is more dilute than the package recommendations.

The slipper orchids in cultivation are of the genus Paphiopedilum, coming from Asia, and are now called "paphs" although for years they were called "cyps" and listed as Cypripedium, which correctly covers the slipper orchids of the North Temperate Zone. A third genus in the slippers is Phragmipedium, the "phrags" being native to Central and South America.

The parts of the flower of a slipper orchid are different in design from other orchids, designated in the diagram of flower parts earlier in the book. The distinguishing features are the pouch-like lip, the broad dorsal sepal at the top, the fusion of the two lateral sepals into one called a synsepalum.

Paphs have been cultivated since the beginning of orchid growing in Europe and many hybrids have been made. The current interest in these orchids has brought a flood of new hybrids onto the scene. Most are classed as "bulldogs", obviously round, fat flowers, but there is much interest in the multifloras, which have several flowers to a stem, perhaps blooming successively, and the unusual species such as Paph. fairieanum and Paph. sukhakulii and their new hybrids. The best known in amateur collections is Paph. Maudiae, green and white. Other favorites include Paph. F.C. Puddle, a small white; yellow-greens such as Golden Diana and Golden Acres; Olivia, a lovely pink.

Landmarks in breeding award-winning paphs by today's standards include Paph. Paeony, Winston Churchill, Farnmoore, and Diversion, to mention only a few.

There is great interest everywhere in the slipper orchids, and don't let anybody tell you that you can't master them unless your conditions are extremely hot and dry. Even then, gadgets can help provide a suitable atmosphere. Hopefully, the next book in this series will be devoted to the slipper orchids.

Pronunciation: Paphiopedilum, "paf -ee-o-PED-i-lum"; Cypripedium, "sip-re-PEE-di-um"; Phragmipedium, "frag-me-PEE-di-um." All the names refer to the slipper-like pouch.

Paphiopedilum Festive Hunter, an attractive hybrid (above). Paphiopedilum sukhakulii, a species, in center below with two of its hybrids.

Dendrobium

(Abbreviation Den.)

Dendrobiums are very popular in many countries because of their variety of blooms, definite growth patterns and eagerness to produce as many flowers as possible.

Some dendrobiums are evergreen, some are deciduous, some are called cane orchids because the pseudobulbs are long and thin. All are sympodial.

Pronounce the name "Den-DRO-bee-um."

Bear in mind that dendrobiums are native to East India, Burma, Southeast Asia and Australia. High humidity and abundant rainfall from June to September characterize this area. The dry season from mid-December to mid-March may be accompanied by bright sunshine.

But since some of the species are native at sea level and others at high elevations, they have varying habits. As a general rule the dendrobiums grow during the summer and flower during the dry season, but Dendrobium phalaenopsis flowers in the fall. Also, as a general rule, these plants take definite rest periods when less water and lower temperatures are desirable to maintain dormancy.

Most grow best in very small pots to the point of being top heavy so the compost dries out rapidly — air circulation is important.

There are about a thousand species and many hybrids in this genus. Some are monsters and some are miniatures.

If you understand the wishes and habits of the types you have and can provide suitable conditions, your dendrobiums will reward you with beautiful and numerous flowers. Some blooms are fleeting, others last for weeks and weeks.

Because the dendrobiums are so varied, you could make a whole collection of them and have lovely and different flowers practically around the calendar.

DENDROBIUM NOBILE — These plants grow rapidly during

Dendrobium Carole Curry, a deep magenta hybrid of the Dendrobium phalaenopsis type, blooms in the fall.

the summer, then need a definite period of dryness and chilling in the fall, similar to that in the Himalayas where they are native. Then a warming up period in late January will make buds pop out all along the stems to cover the plants with blooms in March and April.

They can take temperatures down almost to freezing, if kept dry. But bear in mind that "keeping dry" calls for high humidity and some water and not complete dryness. They like a lot of light all the time.

People in Hawaii take nobile dendrobiums from sea level up the mountains in the fall to chill them and harden them off.

DENDROBIUM PHALAENOPSIS — The species name is very confusing because it is the same as the genus Phalaenopsis. The plants are no kin, but flowers of these dendrobiums have the shape of phalaenopsis flowers.

Many fine hybrids have been made, with emphasis on the pure whites and the very dark reddish-lavenders. Flowers are produced on long sprays from the tops of the bulbs, and contrary to cattleyas, the same bulbs will bloom season after season.

If you have been to Bangkok and have seen the numerous plants grown hanging on porches of houses along the klongs, you know that everybody can grow these orchids.

The seedlings may begin to bloom with a few flowers when the bulbs are only six inches tall; specimen plants may be three or four feet in height with dozens of blooms on many spikes.

They frequently make keikis at the top of the bulbs because the dormant eyes on the stem can produce plants or flowers. Keikis may be removed and potted when they show roots.

Frequent watering and misting during growth should be reduced drastically when the bulbs are mature, but even during rest the plants needs spraying overhead and water in the pots, but less often than during growth. New growth begins in the spring.

EVERGREEN DENDROBIUMS — This group includes a vast number of hybrids derived from crossings of Den. stratiotes, Den. schulleri, Den. veratrifolium, Den. gouldii and others. Some which have narrow, wavy, upright petals are called antelope orchids because of these horns.

These are mostly very tall plants; the canes may be three feet or more in height. The flower spikes are long and long lasting. Flowers have a wide color range, including mustard, white, green, yellow and purple.

If the potting medium is as porous as it should be, almost daily watering is necessary, plus overhead misting in warm weather.

OTHER DENDROBES — Dendrobium aggregatum has small bulbs, single leathery leaves, and flowers like showers of gold coins.

Dendrobium cucumerinum is called "cucumber orchid" because the one-inch pimply leaves look like gherkins, and the related, creeping Den. linguiforme has small leaves like flat green fingernails. Both have whitish flowers with narrow segments.

Dendrobium speciosum, called "rock lily" in its native Australia, grows in huge clumps on rocks in open places in full sun, has long sprays of numerous creamy flowers.

Dendrobium smilliae has flowers so arranged that it is called "bottlebrush orchid," and Den. secundum has an inflorescence like a purple toothbrush!

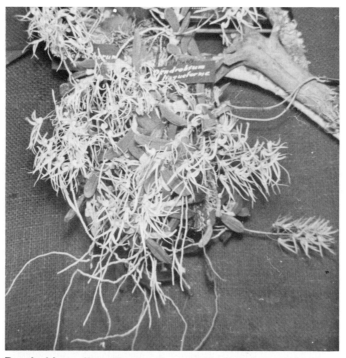

Dendrobium linguiforme is called "tongue orchid" or "thumbnail orchid" because of its flat round leaves. It is an Australian species that grows in masses on rocks or trees.

Miltonia

(Milt.)

Miltonias are called "pansy orchids" because of their roundish, flat flowers, but the pansy orchids are larger than the annual pansies.

There are two groups, the Colombian hybrids termed cool growing and the Brazilian hybrids termed warm growing. However, all of them prefer cool nights because they are native to high elevations in South America.

The plants have thin leaves, unlike the thick succulent foliage of many orchids, which curve gracefully from flat light green pseudobulbs. Bright light is needed to keep the foliage a normal and healthy light green color, but high humidity, moving air, and frequent watering are needed to keep it from excessive evaporation.

Miltonias have fine roots and need to be grown in clumps in pots that might seem too small, repotted only when necessary during the cool season.

Potting mixtures should drain rapidly so that frequent watering keeps the roots damp but never too wet. Fertilizing is done only when plants are in active growth unless the potting mixture contains fir bark.

Miltonias come in lovely colors, some flowers being solid color, others having distinct, and often contrasting, masks in the center. Red, pink, white, yellow, mauve and combinations are charming.

Miltonia Anne Warne, a hybrid of the Brazilian Milt. spectabilis, is a famous Hawaiian hybrid that does beautifully in warm climates, as does its hybrid with Milt. regnellii, Milt. Guanabara. Similar crosses will grow with cattleyas and other orchids in a mixed collection.

Also suitable for warm climates are the many crosses, mostly made in Hawaii, of Milpasia (Miltonia x Aspasia), Milpilia (Miltonia x Trichopilia), Miltassia (Brassia x Miltonia), and Miltonidium (Miltonia and Oncidium).

Bigenerics for cooler climates include Withnerara (Aspasia x Oncidium x Odontoglossum x Miltonia), and Vuylstekera (Cochlioda x Miltonia x Odontoglossum).

**Huntleya meleagris from Co-
lombia h a s d e e p reddish-
orange lacquered flowers with
white centers.**

Odontoglossum
(Odm.)

Odontoglossums are cool orchids with spectacular flowers.

The species from the Colombian Andes, such as Odm. crispum, need protection from extremes in temperature. Wild plants grow at about 60 degrees in airy, buoyant but damp atmosphere, and are subjected to cold temperatures in winter and warm easterly winds in the summer. But in hot weather the plants are shaded by overhead foliage from the direct sun, refreshed by frequent thundershowers which keep them from drying out, and fanned by moving air.

Ideal temperatures range from 50-65°F. degrees at night, with the seasons; 60-70° by day, and 75° during warm daytime weather. They can stand up to 80° if sprayed overhead several times daily, and kept shaded. In cool weather they like filtered sunlight, but not in summer, so if you leave on a vacation, put your odonts under the bench but arrange for somebody to water them.

Odontoglossums dislike being disturbed at their roots. It is better to repot only in January and to repot every year, allowing for

Oncidium cebolleta is a rattail type from South America.

only one new growth, shifting the plants without breaking up the root balls. The plants actually do best when they are almost over the side of the pot so they dry out rapidly.

If leaves curl, this is a danger sign that plants are transpiring water faster than they are taking it up. Raise the humidity when this happens, to reduce evaporation.

The Odontoglossum crispum hybrids seem to be most critical of their environment. Other types adjust quite well if conditions are reasonably satisfactory.

The Central American species, like the yellow and brown Odm. grande, are easier for warm climate collections, as are some of the bigeneric hybrids, especially some of the Odontocidiums (Odontoglossum x Oncidium).

Oncidium

(Abbreviation Onc.)

The delightful "dancing ladies" of the orchid world are the cheerful oncidiums. Most of the flowers, which vary in size from minute to three or four inches, have large lips like swirling yellow ballet skirts. Many are produced in great numbers on long spikes, some of which branch and bloom again after the first flush is over.

Most oncidiums grow well in close quarters in any of the usual mixes providing the potting medium dries out completely between waterings. Many of the types that prefer drier conditions thrive on cork bark slabs or tree fern logs. Most can be grown in mixed

Oncidium ampliatum has branched spikes of yellow "dancing lady" orchids.

collections with only a few, such as Onc. varicosum, needing cool conditions.

There are roughly four groups of these tropical American orchids, a large genus comprising about seven hundred species.

BULBOUS — These have definite pseudobulbs but varying leaves. Onc. onustum has small rounded bulbs and must be grown dry; Oncidium sphacelatum has tall, flattish light green bulbs and thin, long leaves; Onc. ampliatum has round, flat bulbs and very thick leaves.

RATTAIL — Pendulous terete leaves of the "rattail" oncidiums generally indicate that plants grow where conditions are dry. Onc. cebolleta has pencil-size leaves that are dark brownish-green, a foot or longer, with bulbs that are just nubs at the base. We found it growing in a low altitude in Bolivia, a fairly dry area, near the ground on oak trees. In our greenhouse it hangs out of direct range of the mist sprinklers attached to cork bark slabs. Oncidium jonesianum is another rattail with three-inch flowers having bizarre markings and large white lips. We found it in the same area. It should be grown dry.

MULE EAR — These oncidiums have very heavy, pointed, wide leaves that top small, squatty bulbs. Onc. splendidum is familiar, puts up yard-long-spikes of large, bright blooms in winter. Onc. papilio is of this type, has very long flower spikes with single butterfly blooms at a time at the ends. Tiny mule ears are Onc. pumilum, the freckled leaves only an inch or two long, the blooms tiny in branched clusters.

VARIEGATA — Also called "equitant," plants of this group have their little leaves (one to four inches in length) arranged like fans. The lovely little flowers in white, yellow, pink, brown and variations are produced on slender spikes that may be 12 inches long.

Native to the Caribbean, these miniatures grow in rather dry areas. They do best on slabs, and are excellent for windowsill culture because of the diminutive size and colorful blooms.

Onc. variegatum, Onc. triquetrum and Onc. pulchellum are noted.

examples, and many hybrids with these and other species have been made.

Epidendrum

(Epi.)

Epidendrums are kin to cattleyas. They comprise a vast genus found in tropical and sub-tropical American regions with Epi. conopseum growing as far up as North Carolina. There may be a thousand species.

Because of the size and diversity of these orchids, it is impossible to lump them descriptively or culturally. Some grow in rain forests and some in dry areas; some have tiny flowers and some are quite large. But most are easy to grow and floriferous.

Epidendrum conopseum (left) is native to the SE U.S. Tiny green flowers called "green fly" orchid. Epidendrum stamfordianum (right) from Central America has yellow blooms dotted with red.

There are two major groups.

REED-STEM — Epi. ibaguense, commonly called Epi. radicans, grows in full sun in warm climates, has tall slender stems with clusters of flowers from the top, the tiny blooms in a wide range of bright and pastel colors.

Others of this group are identified by their lack of pseudobulbs, their tall upright stems and terminal flower spikes. The leaves alternate along the stems. Epi. pseudepidendrum is a favorite because of its green and orange flowers.

ENCYCLIA — Some botanists make a separate genus of Encyclia, the bulbous epis. Favored in this group are Epi. atropurpureum, with mouse brown wavy sepals and petals, a white or magenta lip; Epi. cochleatum, with a lip like a shell marked with black; Epi mariae, used in hybridizing for the green of its sepals and petals; and Epi. tampense, a small greenish native of Florida and the Bahamas being used to make hybrids of Epicattleyas and Epilaelias and Epilaeliocattleyas that might be hardy enough for outdoor culture north of the usual year-round range of the cattleya types.

... And More

The above major cultivated genera don't include many fascinating orchids that you will see in shows and greenhouses and may wish to grow.

Consider the African species, the exotic angraecums and leopard-spotted ansellias; the green swans, Cycnoches chlorochilon; the curious stanhopeas that bloom from the bottom of the container; the miniature pleurothallis; the curious bulbophyllums, especially Bulbophyllum medusae; the vining vanillas, source of flavoring; and the cool climate masdevallias, with flowers like brightly colored little kites dancing in the wind.

Or, make a collection of oddities that take your fancy, perhaps from among the maxillarias, coelogynes or catasetums. You have an enormous variety of flowers from which to choose the ones that please you.

Angraecum leonis has glistening white flowers with the spur curved like a hairpin. The leaves are folded together so the tropical rain of Grande Comore Island, where it grows, runs off rapidly.

Terrestrial Orchids

Many native orchids in North America are terrestrials, and reference to a wildflower book will show you that many of the roadside, bog and meadow flowers in your area are orchids.

Our native orchids are usually difficult to grow in cultivation, but terrestrials from other countries are more amenable including species of Phaius, Calanthe, Spathoglottis and Peristeria.

Phaius tankervilliae, terrestrial orchids easily grown as pot plants. Patio of Mrs. Frank D. Bisbee, Sr. See color painting of flowers page 73.

This rare Madagascan species (above) has two-inch olive green flowers dangling from four-foot thread-like stems. It is Aeranthes neoperrieri 'Hazel' CBM/AOS. (Below), Aerangis citrata from the same area has creamy one-inch blooms strung along pendant stems.

Yellow phalaenopsis and cream, yellow and gold cattleyas with Jerusalem oak and orange grapes in a copper bowl on a gold base. Design by Mrs. Truman Green.

CHAPTER V

PROPAGATION

There are two ways to propagate (multiply) plants. By seed, which is the sexual method of placing pollen from one flower onto another. And by vegetative means, by which a new plant is produced from another plant.

Vegetative Propagation

BACK BULBS — When a sympodial plant has enough bulbs to support a new growth, plus two or three inactive but still green bulbs at the back of the plant, the back bulbs may be encouraged to grow into a new plant.

If left alone, they may not make any new growth but gradually turn brown and die as they give support to the active bulbs. But if cut from the front part of the plant, they make every effort to stay alive.

There are two ways to do this.

One is at the time of repotting. When the plant is cleaned of all the old potting material, count the bulbs and decide where the division is to be made. Cut through the rhizome with a sharp knife. Then pot the front part in the usual manner.

The back bulbs probably have no roots, which doesn't matter. But they must have one good green eye.

Don't pot up the back bulbs. Instead, stand them up in a pot of damp sphagnum moss or lay them on a flat of damp sand. Set in a shady place, like under the greenhouse bench, and spray them with water once or twice daily on sunny days. When an eye begins to swell or roots to form, pot them up as usual. It is ncessary to use a stake that clips to the side of the pot and to tie them securely with plastic wire so they don't wobble or fall out of the pot.

Another method is to put the back bulbs into plastic bags. Put into the bottom of each bag a handful of wet sphagnum moss or an egg-sized piece of osmunda, something to hold moisture. Make a couple of holes with a pencil about halfway up the bag to allow for a little air circulation.

Tie the bag shut at the top with wire, and hang it on the side of the greenhouse bench. In warm weather(unless your climate is very dry) hang the bag outdoors in the shade.

Check every week, and add water if the inside of the bag is not moist. Use bags large enough so leaves and all are enclosed.

Another way is to use a bag without airholes, choosing a smaller size. Put about an inch of water in the bottom, insert the bulbs, and tie the bag shut around the bulbs with the leaves protruding.

If you want to divide a plant which does not need repotting that year, use the second system.

Simply cut through the rhizome to sever front from back, but do not disturb the bulbs. Leave both parts intact in the pot. The back bulbs will put out new growths, if all goes well, and may be potted separately when the front needs repotting.

Back bulbs may not flower on the first growth, which may be smaller than usual. Even when it does bloom the first time, the flower may not be up to par, but when the back division attains full size, then the flowers should be exactly like those on front divisions.

Cymbidium back bulbs are leafless and may be at the back or in the center of a clump. When repotting a large clump after flowering, shake off all the soil, and cut through the rhizome.

Insert the back bulbs one- third their depth into a flat of fine fir bark, peat moss, sand, or pea gravel. Keep shady and moist until

DIVISIONS AND PROPAGATIONS

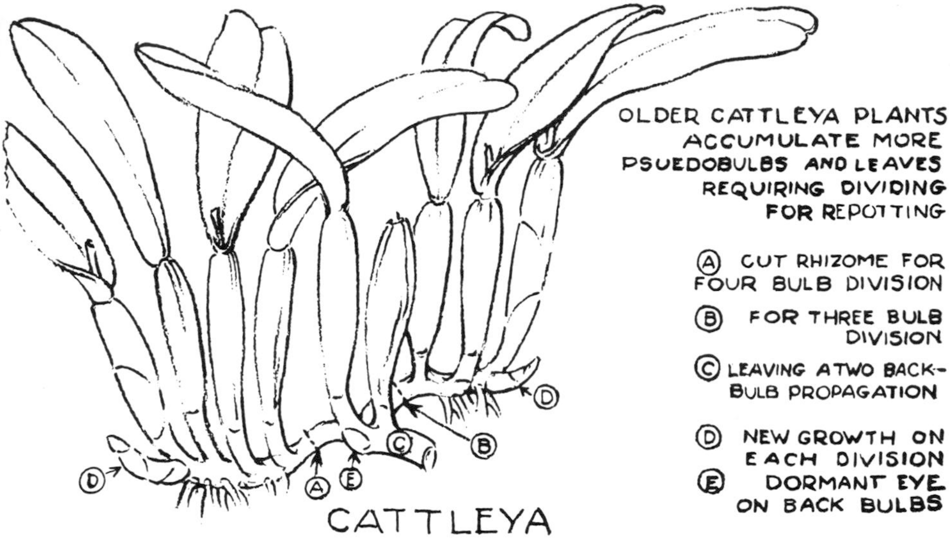

OLDER CATTLEYA PLANTS
ACCUMULATE MORE
PSUEDOBULBS AND LEAVES
REQUIRING DIVIDING
FOR REPOTTING

(A) CUT RHIZOME FOR FOUR BULB DIVISION

(B) FOR THREE BULB DIVISION

(C) LEAVING A TWO BACK-BULB PROPAGATION

(D) NEW GROWTH ON EACH DIVISION

(E) DORMANT EYE ON BACK BULBS

CATTLEYA

(A) CUT FOR TOP DIVISION

(B) KEIKI (BABY PLANTS)

VANDA

(A) PLANTLETS GROWING FROM NODES CUT OFF AND POT SEPARATELY—

DENDROBIUM

BRUNO ALBERTS

Renanthera Brookie Chandler. Monopodial orchids are propagated by top cuttings and keikis.

new growth and roots are evident. Then pot up into your regular mixture in a pot large enough for three years' growth, as it may take this long for back bulbs to flower.

When cutting a rhizome of any type orchid, dust the cut surface with a fungicide dust. On cymbidiums, paint the wound with tree seal. Always use sterilized tools.

DIVISIONS — A mature sympodial plant that is making two new leads simultaneously and has three or four bulbs to support each one may be divided into two separate plants which may be expected to flower regularly without interruption. Back bulbs may be cut off at the same time.

A portion of a plant with an active lead is called a division to distinguish it from back bulbs. Be sure, if you are buying "a piece" of a fine plant, that you understand if it is a front division or a back bulb propagation.

Cymbidiums may be divided into two or more divisions at re-potting time. Front divisions should have three to seven bulbs, and the best flowering comes from large plants. Here, too, it may be possible to get two or three front divisions plus some back bulbs.

Not all orchids require several bulbs in a division. Cycnoches, for example, can grow and flower from a single bulb.

TOP CUTTINGS — Some of the monopodial orchids, notably reed-stem epidendrums and vandas, may be propagated by top cuttings.

When a plant is tall enough to be divided, simply cut off the top, a portion having at least six pairs of leaves and a few aerial roots.

Leave the bottom piece alone. It will sprout, but of course it will make new growth from the side of the stem and will never be perfectly symmetrical as it was before.

Pot up the top cutting as you would an established plant, and keep it misted frequently until it has several good roots of its own.

Phalaenopsis may be propagated by top cuttings, but the method is different and does not always result in more than one plant if the base does not sprout again.

When a mature phalaenopsis plant has developed a trunk-like stem a few inches above the potting material, and has new roots at the upper portion of this stem below the leaves, you can cut off the top portion. This can be done only if it has new roots with it that have not yet penetrated the rooting medium. Timing is everything.

Take the top, which is all the leaves plus a few new roots, and pot just as you do any mature phalaenopsis.

Leave the bottom part strictly alone. Do not repot it. Set it in a shady place, and keep the medium dry. Keep humidity up, but do not water the pot more than about once in two weeks.

Eventually a dormant eye within the stump should begin to grow and a new little plant appear. When the new plant has roots about an inch long, cut it loose where it joins the stump, pot it up and treat as a seedling.

Still leave the stump alone and treat as before, as a second and maybe a third and fourth plant will develop, depending on the age and condition of the stump. This process can be used only with large, old plants.

OFFSETS — Offsets are little plants that grow off some part of a mature plant, generally without artificial stimulation.

Dendrobiums frequently produce these little plants from the nodes (joints) on the canes. On an upright cane, slice the plantlet loose from the parent when the baby has a few roots and is a few inches tall. Pot separately and treat as a seedling.

On the pendant type dendrobiums, such as Den. pierardii, numerous offsets may form on the canes. Since the canes are pliable, merely curve the cane around to the potting medium in which it is growing, and attach the offset by stapling down the cane with a hairpin. When the offset puts its roots into the log or potting medium, cut it loose from the cane. It may be necessary to slice a piece off the cane.

Some phalaenopsis, especially of the Phal. lueddemanniana group, make offsets on the long flower stem, which may be cut off when they have roots, or curled back and anchored with hairpins.

Vanda keikis (keiki, pronounced "cake-y," is the Hawaiian word for baby) may be severed from parent plants or left alone to form a colony.

Orchids From Seeds

Some people are afraid to grow orchids because they think they have to wait seven years for the first flower.

But of course, amateurs don't begin by buying seeds. They don't grow roses from seeds do they?

So, the answer for beginners is to buy mature plants in bud or bloom. And when they become experienced in culture, they can get smaller seedlings and grow them to maturity. Many amateur growers

**This catasetum has separate male and fe-
male flowers. Most orchids have both sexes
fused in the column of each flower.**

do grow orchids from seeds, once they have a sufficient collection
of flowering size plants, but many others prefer to have more variety
by choosing several different seedlings from various nurseries than
to give space to a great number all of one kind.

SEED — Two orchids are carefully selected as parents, chosen
for specific qualities of the flowers. Hand pollination results, if
successful, in formation of a seed pod.

FLASKS — When the pod is mature (this may take several months) or while still green (this method is called embryo culture), the tiny dustlike seeds are planted in a solution of nutrients inside a sterile glass bottle under the most antiseptic conditions. Orchid seeds are without their own food supply. Beans, for instance, feed their sprouts from the fleshly part of the beans until roots and leaves can function. Orchid seeds are planted into special mixtures (which may contain coconut milk, sugar and other ingredients) and sealed inside the bottles.

Eventually, if all goes well, green fuzz on top the agar (planting medium) can be distinguished as individual plants. Flasks may be transplanted (reflasked) once or twice.

COMMUNITY POTS — When the tiny plants are big enough to come out of their incubators, they are planted into community pots, so called because a dozen or more seedlings are in one pot. The medium is of fine texture. The pots are kept damp and shaded.

SEEDLINGS — As the seedlings grow they are advanced through the various pot sizes until they reach maturity.

Growing seedlings under lights for longer days, and with carefully controlled conditions may bring them into bloom quicker than the legendary seven years. Some genera mature faster than that normally.

Chromosomes

The words chromosome, tetraploid, and other unfamiliar terms turn up with increasing frequency in articles and even advertisements for orchids.

These are matters which concern people who are hybridizing orchids. Chromosomes are minute bodies within the nucleus of the cells of plants, animals and people. They determine the characteristics of the offspring. Chromosomes may be counted only in cells which are dividing (such as active root tips), and seen only through microscopes.

What you need to understand are the terms and how plants might differ because their chromosomes are different.

For instance, the haploid (or basic) number of chromosomes in a cattleya is 20, so a normal cattleya has 40 chromosomes (written 2N because 40 is 2 x 20) in each tiny cell because it gets 20 from each parent.

The word poly means many, so any plant with more than the usual number is a polyploid.

A triploid is 3N or 3 x 20, so it has 60 chromosomes.

A tetraploid is 4N or 4 x 20, having 80 chromosomes.

A pentaploid is 5N or 5 x 20, and has 100 chromosomes.

A hexaploid is 6N or 6 x 20, having 120 chromosomes.

Now, what does this mean to you?

Diploids grow well, and a diploid flower fertilized with the pollen of another diploid flower produces diploid seedlings. Diploids each have 40 chromosomes, but their offspring do not have 80 because

White phalaenopsis produce beautiful flowers on long sprays. Phalaenopsis Scotti Maguire.

during the growth process the cells keep dividing and dividing the chromosomes to maintain the same number throughout.

A diploid (40) will mate with a tetraploid (80) to produce a triploid (60). Triploids may have fine flowers but often are sterile and useless for breeding.

Tetraploids (4N equals 80) often have fine flowers and are vigorous plants. They combine with other teraploids to make another generation of tetraploids.

Pentaploids (5N equals 100) are rather rare because they may result from the crossing of a tetraploid and a hexaploid.

A word you do not often see but which enters into this multiplication table is aneuploid. An aneuploid is one which has some odd number of chromosomes rather than a conventional multiple. Such plants are poor growers and may die in the flask or before they are mature enough to bloom.

You cannot look at a plant and determine the number of chromosomes, but if you are buying from catalogs or ads which list seedlings from parents whose chromosomes have been counted, then you have some idea of what to expect.

However, is its well to remember that not all polyploids are going to produce award quality flowers, but that very often flowers which are prize winners have more than the usual number of chromosomes. (Pronounce this "CROW-mow-som" so each syllable rhymes.) Incidentally, normal people have 46 chromosomes. The basic number for camellia plants is 15, or 2N equals 30 in the diploids. There is a basic number of chromosomes for each genus. The diploid species of Phalaenopsis count at 38, so the basic number is 19.

Mericlones

There are plants available that are called meristems or mericlones. These are vegetative divisions from one mature plant, and as such carry the varietal name and the award, if any, given to the mother plant. There may be thousands of mericlones grown from a single plant, all identical.

For meristem culture a tiny piece of plant tissue is extracted from a growing point within the mother plant. It is put into sterile bottles with agar, like seeds are, and continually cut into small pieces as it grows. The proliferations can be made indefinitely, but when cutting is stopped the tiny pieces develop into plants.

Not all genera of orchids have been meristemmed with success yet, but the process is being developed for more genera all the time.

The flowers are identical to those of the parent plant and so, with mericlones, you can have plants of fine quality at small cost. You must grow them well to realize their full potential.

Mericlones supplement, but do not replace, seedlings in a collection. Mericlones are from older hybrids, since the mother plant must be mature and then the mericlones grown to maturity, whereas many seedlings offer new departures and improvements on established types.

For more meristem culture see "You Can Grow Cattleya Orchids," a sequel to this book.

Vanda Rothschildiana, a famous blue strapleaf which blooms several times a year.

Many fine cattleya hybrids have been meristemmed and are available at reasonable prices. (Top) Blc. Orange Glory 'Empress' AM/AOS, FCC/RHS; (Center) Bc. Deesse 'Charles' PC/RHS; (Lower) Blc. Ermine 'Lines' AM/AOS.

CHAPTER VI

PROBLEMS

Orchid plants are tough, and are not appetizing to many garden pests, but alas, there are some who think them delicious.

Fortunately, such serious pests as the cattleya fly, dendrobium beetle and others, found where orchids grow wild, are rare in cultivation. The importance of observing quarantine regulations cannot be exaggerated. Sneak in one plant and you may bring some pest that will ruin your collection.

There are three points of great importance.

One, IDENTIFY YOUR PROBLEM, then choose a control which specifies that it takes care of scale, snails or whatever you have. It is a waste of your time and money to treat a pest with some chemical which does not exterminate him, or to use a pesticide when a fungicide is needed for disease.

Two, USE ANY PRODUCT EXACTLY AS DIRECTED ON THE LABEL. Read every word before applying. Mix in exact proportions, as specified. Apply precisely as directed, at the stated intervals. TWICE AS MUCH IS NOT TWICE AS GOOD, and you may injure your plants. All these products have been carefully checked out by the companies that market them, and you must follow directions if you wish to get results.

Three, TAKE ALL PRECAUTIONS ADVISED, and then some. Remember that anything that will kill an insect is poison. Never, never smoke when spraying. All you need is to get a drop of poison on your cigarette and inhale it. Wear coverup clothes (not shorts), long sleeves, something on your head, and, if recommended, gloves and glasses. Don't rub your eyes, or eat, or anything before you change clothes and bathe.

Application is easy now. Many preparations may be applied with gadgets attached to the garden hose. Others come in aersol cans or plastic squeeze cans. Some products contain combinations of insecticide, fungicide and miticide.

Systemic chemicals are absorbed by the plant tissue and are effective for a period of time.

We are not giving recommendations by product names as products and government regulations change too rapidly. If you need advice, consult your local agricultural officials. For help in identifying pests, consult the illustrations in "You Can Grow Cattleya Orchids" and "You Can Grow Phalaenopsis Orchids."

The Pests

SCALE — This is the most common and worrisome pest on cattleyas and their allies. Scale insects are white, the young ones like white powder, the mature ones tiny round pinheads. There are also brown and red scales.

These are sucking insects which collect on tender growths, particularly under the tissue covering on the bulbs, around the dormant eyes, and under the strings that tie up a plant. They do not attack flowers, but a bulb weakened by scale cannot flower properly.

SNAILS, SLUGS — These are chewing pests that work by night, generally within the potting mixture. They feast on roots, sometimes climb up to chew new growths and even flowers and flower spikes.

Bush snails are tiny, brown, pinhead-size creatures which multiply rapidly and may do enormous root damage before you even know they are there.

Larger snails of several sizes, and slugs, which are snails without shells, leave slimy trails. Keep your greenhouse clean, as these creatures hide under debris as well as in pots.

Use bait for large snails and slugs, putting it on coke bottle caps and setting these on the potting mixture. For bush snails, use a drench. Apply to potting medium thoroughly until it runs out the bottom.

If you tie a piece of cotton around your flower spikes below the blooms, snails and slugs cannot crawl over it.

SOWBUGS, MILLIPEDES, EARTHWORMS, SPRINGTAILS — These are problems in the pots and should be attacked with a drench, as above.

ROACHES — Cockroaches happily inhabit heated greenhouses, orchid pots or hanging baskets. They emerge at night to eat blooms or feed in the compost. Use any household poison specified for roaches between the pots, not the potting mix or on the plants.

ANTS, TERMITES — Ants may nest in a pot without your knowledge until you water heavily and they run to the surface. If you are suspicious, immerse the pot in a bucket of water, or empty it out. A complete repotting job is necessary to remove the eggs.

Tiny little sugar ants may appear on flower buds to eat the honey at the tips, but do no damage.

Termites get in greenhouse wood frames or benches, so use redwood or cedar for building. Do not use professional termite extermination sprays in your home or greenhouse without removing all of the plants, as fumes from some of these materials are deadly to plants as well. Better yet, build your greenhouse of termite-proof wood.

GRASSHOPPERS, RATS, MICE, SQUIRRELS — Any of these intruders may do damage to plants and flowers. If they are bad problems in warm climates, it may be necessary to screen the growing area.

MEALYBUGS, APHIDS, THRIPS — Mealybugs you can see, as they are white, powdery ovals. They gather in clusters multiply rapidly in warm weather, and suck juices from leaves and flower stems.

Aphids are nearly invisible, clustering on flower buds and new growths. They may be of different colors.

Thrips are so tiny they are difficult to see, but are common garden pests and usually attack flowers, causing deformities.

There are a number of preparations under various trade names for these pests, both contact and systemic. Observe precautions about spraying flowers. If yours is a small collection and the mealybugs are few, you can dip a matchstick tipped with cotton into any alcohol solution or nail polish remover and touch them with it.

MITES — Mites are sucking insects which collect on new growth, on the undersides of leaves, and multiply like mad in dry weather. They dislike being wet, so spraying water on the undersides of the foliage discourages (but doesn't control) them. You may not know mites are there until the color begins to disappear from the foliage. If you inspect the undersides of the leaves, you may be able to see tiny pinprick dots, especially in the case of red spiders (which are mites) which look like red pepper, and spin fine webs.

There are several good miticides available, and a specific mite control is necessary.

The Diseases

Diseases are harder to diagnose and control than pests, as virus in plants is just as mysterious as virus in people.

This is why it is important to diagnose the trouble, as an insecticide will do nothing to cure a disease. Keeping insects under control may help prevent some diseases, however, as some are transmitted from plant to plant by insects.

Good healthy plants grown in clean, ventilated areas will escape some of the diseases that plague crowded plants in weak condition.

Isolation of diseased plants is important. Throw them out if the disease is positively identified.

Sterilization of your potting tools is important. You can transmit a virus to dozens of plants after cutting one diseased plant with

Every flower on an African "leopard orchid" has a different pattern of spots. This is Ansellia gigantea var. azanica
'McQuerry' HCC/AOS. See color painting page 76.

your knife. And when you discard a diseased plant, throw away
pot, stakes, everything.

FUNGUS DISEASES — Black rot often occurs during periods
of low temperatures, caused by collection of moisture in crevices.
Cattleya type plants may collect water in new leads that are open at
the top. Pulling away the outer brown bulb covering allows water
to run out. If rot develops, cut back to healthy tissue and treat with
a fungicide. Phalaenopsis may get rot if water collects in the crowns,
and for this reason some growers hang plants sideways so water
runs out.

Soil fungus may attack cymbidiums at the base of old or new growths. Such rot may be caused by standing water or by not drying off the plants before night in chilly, dull weather.

Mycelium, a thread-like fungus, and snow mold invade potting mixtures, make the mixture difficult to keep wet and smother the roots. Repotting is necessary, with roots completely cleaned of old mix and dipped in fungicide. Root rot disease is caused by mycelium fungus and infected roots, bulbs and leaves should be cut off beyond the infection.

Seedlings are subject to damp-off and should be treated regularly with a fungicide that helps to prevent the disease.

Rusts may be identified as orange or orange and black pustules on the leaves, upper, lower or both surfaces. Cut off and burn the infected portion.

BACTERIAL DISEASES — A leaf spotting disease of phalaenopsis begins with a small discolored ring spot and spreads through one leaf and then through the whole plant. Various fungicides have been used with varying success.

Soft rot of cattleyas may begin with watery spots on the foliage which spread and turn the leaf into a black, wet mass which smells. It can begin in bulbs or rhizomes. Cut off the infected portion back to green tissue and keep plant dry and away from overhead spraying. Disinfect your cutting tools or you will spread the disease.

Soft rot of cymbidiums is characterized by soft tissues and unpleasant odor. Bareroot the plant, cut off affected parts and soak the good portion in fungicide. Repot in fresh compost.

Brown rot of paphiopedilums begins on a leaf with a watery spot and spreads rapidly. This disease is encouraged by high temperature, high humidity, and may be spread by overhead watering.

Miltonia leaf scorch begins at the tips of the leaves and spreads by orangeish streaks through foliage and bulbs. Cool the house and cut off the infected portion of the plant.

VIRUS DISEASES — Cymbidium mosaic virus is not limited to cymbidiums but infects many other genera. The symptoms may not be noticeable, and may vary. Streaking or mottling, or flecking of the leaves may indicate virus. Cutting tools transmit this virus from plant to plant, and unless you sterilize your knife after cutting each plant and flower, you spread it through your collection. Plants which show no diseases symptoms but flower and grow poorly even if well treated may be victims of this diseases.

Color break virus causes flowers to be irregular in color, sometimes distorted in form. One flower that is irregular, such as having lip color on a sepal, may not indicate color break virus, but if flowers are streaked or mottled a second time, the plant is suspect. Unless it is a stud (which may not transmit the virus to its seedlings), you would do well to discard the plant. The same damage may be caused by thrips rather than virus.

If you maintain a preventive program, you might spray your plants about once a month with a broad-spectrum insecticide and then with a fungicide or bactericide. Water plants thoroughly before applying chemicals, even those mixed with water for application.

Friends

If you grow orchids in a warm climate, you have some very helpful garden and greenhouse friends to help you eradicate the pests. Chameleons eat insects all day long, do no damage to plants or flowers. Toads hop around at night cleaning up the nocturnal pests. Take care of your friends, and watch out for them when spraying with poison.

Little green tree frog sitting on a phalaenopsis leaf is a friend in the greenhouse. He eats insects.

Our greenhouse (Mary and Jack McQuerry) is a prefabricated glass house 15 x 32 feet from Texas Greenhouse Co. It has two aisles, three benches and many plants hanging above. We grow many genera of orchids in this greenhouse. Automatic equipment takes care of the environment with a minimum of attention from us.

CHAPTER VII

HOUSING

The thought of orchids brings to mind a vision of a beautiful big greenhouse. Yet, the large number of home gardeners who are growing orchids indicates that expensive equipment is not necessary.

Nowadays people are growing orchids in large and small greenhouses, in kitchen and bathroom windows, in family rooms and glass-enclosed porches, in high-rise condominiums and apartments, basements and attics. Growing under artificial light is increasingly popular as the techniques and equipment improve.

Greenhouses

The easiest way to control the climate around an orchid collection is in a greenhouse.

The size of the house depends upon space available in the yard, the number of plants on hand, and the number anticipated. No matter how big you build it, your greenhouse will fill up fast.

A greenhouse offers endless pleasure, because you can work with your plants at night, during bad weather, on dreary winter evenings.

Even in a warm climate, a greenhouse grows plants well, especially if it has cooling and humidifying gadgets. It permits you to control the amount of light and shade, water and wind, as well as temperature and humidity.

We have lots of oaks and pine trees in our neighborhood but the greenhouse gets bright morning and midday sun.

There are a great many prefabricated greenhouses on the market today in lean-to or free-standing designs. It is cheaper in the long run to erect one of these houses than to build your own. The design has such important things as drip grooves to carry off the condensation of moisture, and the right slant to the roof for the most light. The materials are impervious to weather and moisture. If you build your own, you may well find that it leaks, drips and rots and that upkeep is expensive.

Be sure to deal with established greenhouse companies which advertise nationally or regionally, not some local, inexperienced builder.

There are several items to consider when deciding among the prefabs available.

One is, of course, a suitable size for you. If the house comes in sections, you can add to it later.

Another is your climate. If you live in a cold climate you may want a type where the side walls are low and the roof low, to hold in the heat. On the other hand, if your climate gets warm in the summer, you need a style with high side walls which raises the roof well above all plants on the benches and allows for circulation of air. This keeps plants cool, and allows room for hanging plants above those on the benches.

Adequate ventilation is another factor, and there should be ridge vents in both sides of the roof.

Large panes of glass are more resilient than small panes, and less likely to break.

A prefab greenhouse is delivered with all the pieces cut and ready to assemble. Mr. and Mrs. Robert Leslie put their 9 x 12 greenhouse together in a few days.

A prefab greenhouse 9 x
15 feet fits into a city
garden and houses many
orchid plants.

Heating depends on the size of the house and the fuels available
to you. Special greenhouse heaters are built to stand the humid atmosphere, and last longer than home heaters. Any heating system
should be controlled with a thermostat as weather can change
suddenly in the night or when you are not at home.

Cooling in hot weather is desirable, with greenhouse coolers that
add moisture to the air at the same time. A fan to circulate the air
is helpful at all seasons. Orchids are air plants and dislike a stuffy,
stale atmosphere.

Shading in summer is necessary in almost every climate. This may
be applied to the glass with a paint sprayer or rollers, using a type
of shading compound recommended for greenhouse glass. Or, you
may suspend plastic shade cloth on frames above the roof, raising it
high enough so you can open the vents below it.

Where to put your greenhouse is important. Remember that
plants need morning sun, all year, which means making sure the
location gets sun in the winter. You can add shade, but you can't
lighten up a house placed in a shady location.

Benches for orchids should be porous, preferably made of pressed steel or hardware cloth. Be sure the legs are of termite-proof material.

Many genera of orchids can be grown together, and you can achieve this even in a small house by growing the phalaenopsis in the shady end, the vandas hanging from the rafters, the dendrobiums in the sun, the cattleyas in an intermediate situation, and the paphiopedilums near the coolers.

Glass or plastic? Both have advantages, but until the plastics become more durable, glass is less expensive because it does not have to be replaced every few years. If your climate is warm, a plastic house may be too hot unless you have adequate ventilation or cooling equipment. Some plastics turn darker or become brittle with age, and plastic sheeting can be ripped off by wind.

Orchids Outdoors

Where the climate is suitable, orchids are good for landscaping. They can be grown on live trees, driftwood trees, tree fern poles, and in pots or baskets. Great beds of reed-stem epidendrums and terete and semi-terete vandas can landscape a whole tropical garden.

Indoor-outdoor arrangements are useful where the climate is not warm enough all year for orchids outdoors. Hanging plants from trees or using them decoratively with rocks and pebbles during the warm months changes to greenhouse culture for the cold season.

Orchids Indoors

Many people grow orchids in their homes. The temperature is about right, generally, but the humidity and light may be low. Using your brightest east or south window for the growing area may provide enough light. Humidity can be increased by setting the pots on trays filled with pebbles and water, so organized that the pots are above, and not in, the water.

Artificial light for orchids is coming on strong.

The usual arrangement calls for two or three tiers of waterproof shelves with lights suspended above them. Depending on the size of the plants, the lamps are mounted 26 to 32 inches above the bench. You can use cool white and daylight tubes alternately, or use tubes recommended for growing plants.

The length of the day, when the lights are on, is important. Seedlings may be given days as long as 16 hours to keep them growing, but constant long days, or constant short days will inhibit flowering of some mature orchids. Some growers reset their automatic timers about once a month so lights burn from dawn to dusk.

Along with light, plants must have the other elements of water, humidity and congenial temperatures day and night.

The Spaniards called phalaenopsis "mariposas" (butterflies) so a butterfly frame of silver wire is an appropriate background for a single phalaenopsis corsage to be worn in the hair. Design by Mrs. Winona W. Jordan.

CHAPTER VIII

CORSAGES AND ARRANGEMENTS

Enjoy your orchids!

Wear them proudly on any occasion. Use them as cut flowers in your home, even on the breakfast table, or bring flowering plants indoors to be enjoyed, slipping the pots inside decorative containers.

Get a supply of inexpensive bud vases and carry single cattleyas or sprays of orchids to hospital patients or shut-ins, men or women. You don't need foliage, or to make a fancy design. Put a corsage on top of a gift package, or use orchids as gifts on special occasions or to express congratulations. You would be amazed how many women have never had an orchid. You will get a thrill from being the giver of the first one.

And what about a baby? A single phalaenopsis or cymbidium to pin to the bassinet is a distinctive gift.

Any orchids, large or small, convey your message of good will.

Corsages

With all the colors, shapes and sizes available in orchid flowers, there is something for every costume and occasion. Do not make elaborate corsages or overdress your orchids with so much ribbon and net that you do not know where the flowers begin or end. Rib-

Pink phalaenopsis and lavender cattleyas combined with gilded stre-litzia, aspidistra and leatherleaf fern foliage in a line-mass design in a handmade bamboo container on a teak base. Arranged by Mrs. Truman Green.

bon in harmony, properly used, enhances the design, but flowers should always dominate.

The first step is to pick the flowers at the proper time. Most orchids open slowly, and flowers that are picked when still green will not last long. Cymbidiums should be open on the spike for about 10 days before blooms are cut. Cattleyas take four or five days from the time the buds crack until blooms are mature.

Cut the stem with a sharp knife in a slanting cut. Do not use scissors, which pinch the cells together so stems can't absorb water. Put the flowers in water overnight to condition them. Refrigerator temperature (or room temperature) for keeping flowers should be around 50 degrees.

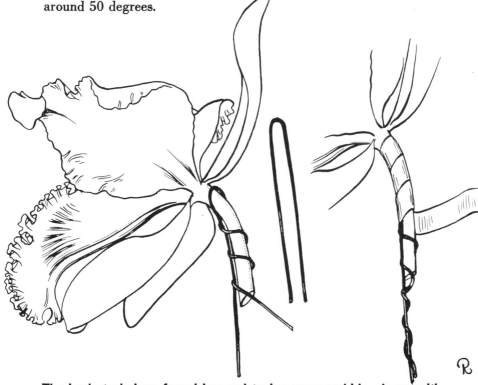

The basic technique for wiring and taping many orchids, shown with a cattleya. Sketches by Marion Ruff Sheehan.

Flowers conditioned for 12 hours or more should hold up for several days without further water.

When you are not wearing a corsage, put it in a box on shredded paper and return it to the refrigerator.

The first step in making a corsage is to wire and tape the stem. The next is to assemble the flowers into a design, if more than one bloom is used. And the third is to add the ribbon or other extraneous material.

The purpose of wiring is to secure the stem, and to substitute lightweight wire for a portion of the bulky flower stem.

Tape hides the wires and protects clothing from the wire ends.

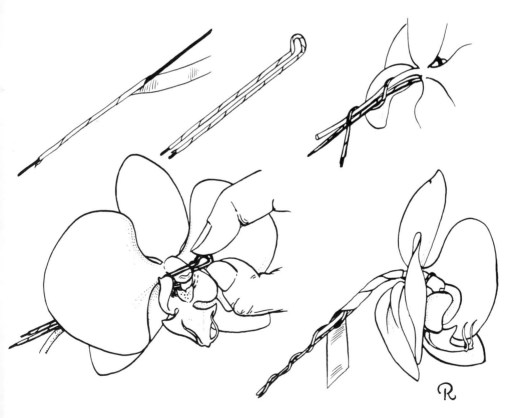

One way to wire phalaenopsis. Sketches by Marion Ruff Sheehan.

Many orchids can be wired by one method. This consists of reducing the stem to one inch, or less in the case of small flowers. Choose wire that is heavy enough but will not break the stem.

Bend the wire through the middle like a hairpin. Put one side against the stem, parallel, with the hairpin curve right up against the back of the flower where the top sepal joins the stem.

Wrap the other half of the wire around and around the stem and the other piece of wire, even below where the stem ends.

For small flowers use a light wire, cover each stem with tape to keep the wire from cutting it, then wire as above.

To tape a flower that has been wired, select floral tape that harmonizes with the bloom. Place one end up at the top of the stem at the back of the flower. Stretching as you go, wrap it around and around to cover the length of the wires.

If using more than one flower, wrap all of them first, having the taped wire stems longer than you think you need. This gives freedom in assembling the design, and any surplus can be cut off. Then arrange the flowers into the design, and fasten the stem together at one or more points.

Phalaenopsis have fragile stems. Take a lightweight wire, cover with floral tape the color of the flower. Shape into a hairpin and bend the curved end on a slight angle (see sketch). Insert this wire through the flower from the front so that the ends pass through the two openings in the center of the flower, and the curve of the hairpin rests on top of the column. Behind the flower, wrap one end around the other as described above.

To make a simple bow, fold one loop at a time and pinch across the ribbon with your fingers as you put the loop in place. Then curve another loop and pinch above the first one. Continue until you have a bow as large as you wish.

Cut off the ribbon, then cut another piece about eight inches long. Still holding the bow in one hand, twist the new piece through the middle and then tie it around where the loops join. Tie tightly. Then put the bow in place and tie the ends of the eight-inch piece around the stems.

Practice your techniques until you can make a corsage that stays together, doesn't wobble, the flowers don't fall out or the taped stem come unwound.

And please place flowers right side up throughout most of the design. You don't want soldiers in a row, but orchids should be worn as they grow, although you may turn a few blooms at slight angles to make the line of the corsage design.

Many orchid shows have competition for corsages and bouquets. You can get ideas from these designs, and enter some of your own work.

Arrangements

Orchids are beautiful in arrangements. You can use them in your home or enter them in a show. Orchids lend themselves to simple or elaborate designs, and you can make interesting arrangements with one cattleya flower or a stem of vandas. As church flowers, orchids are unexcelled.

Many people do not know how to work with orchids. This is because they don't know how they grow and the flowers look distorted when not used right side up.

Because orchid blooms may have short stems, you may need to use florist stakes, orchid tubes or other mechanical aids.

Orchids are versatile. You can use them with other flowers, with foliage, with driftwood, dried materials, and flowering tree branches.

If you are not adept in flower arranging, take a course from your nearest garden club and get some basic books on flower arrangements. The same principles of design that apply to all arrangements should be considered: line, color harmony, form, texture, balance, rhythm, proportion, compatibility of materials, and appropriateness of container.

It isn't difficult to arrange orchids. It just takes practice.

Phalaenopsis are lovely for corsages or bouquets. Above, a bouquet for a bride or bridesmaid of white phalaenopsis, rhynchostylis and b a b y ' s breath backed with fern. Designed by Mrs. J. Frank McClain. Right, three phalaenopsis on hearts of wire covered with silver and white ribbon. Corsage by Mrs. C. C. Curry.

INDEX

Aerangis 99
Aeranthes 76, 99
Aerides 79
Aganisia 65
Angraecum 19, 97
Anguloa 80
Ansellia 76, 117
Arachnis 79
Arrangements of orchids 32, 100, 128, 132
Artificial light 126
Ascocenda 72, 75-78
Ascocentrum 75
Awards 30-31

Back bulbs 101-104
Bacterial disease, see Diseases
Bark 50-51
Baskets, see Containers
Brassavola 60
Brassia 27
Brassocattleya 60, 112
Brassolaeliocattleya 60, 69, 112
Bulb, see Pseudobulb
Bulbophyllum 76

Catasetum 107
Cattleya, culture and hybrids 58-62 illustrations 4, 12, 15, 25, 59, 60, 61, 65, 69, 103
Chromosomes 108-110
Column 25-27
Color break, see Disease
Community pots 108
Containers 52-53
Corsages 126-133
Culture 33-45
Cuttings 105-106
Cycnoches 15
Cymbidium, kinds and culture 15, 25, 62-70, 77
Cypripedium, see Paphiopedilum

Dendrobium 15, 86-89
    illustration 51, 68, 87, 89, 103
Diseases 116-118
Division 104-105
Doritaenopsis 46, 68, 74
Doritis 74

Encyclia 96
Epidendrum 95-96
    illustrations 44, 65, 80, 95
Eye 18

Fertilizer 42-45
Fir bark, see Bark
Flasks 108
Flowers 18, 21-24
Foliage, see Leaf
Friends(lizards, toads, etc.) 119
Fungus, See Diseases

Genus, genera, see Names
Greenhouses 38, 120-125
Hapuu - see Tree Fern
Home growing 125
Housing 120-126
Humidity 39-42
Huntleya 91
Hybrids 28-31, 107-110

Indoor growing 125
Insects, see Pests

Keiki, see Offset

Laelia 58
Laeliocattleya 58, 61, 69
Landscaping 125
Lead 20
Leaf 14, 17
Light 35-36
    artificial 126
Lip 25-26

Ludisia 73

Masdevallia 80
Mediums, potting 49-52
Mericlone, meristem 69, 110-112
Miltonia 25, 65, 90
Monopodial growth 16-21
    propagation 103, 105-106

Names 28-31
Neomoorea 80

Odontoglossum 91-92
Offset 106
Oncidium 15, 93-95
    illustrations 25, 37, 56, 65, 92,
    93
Osmunda 50

Paphiopedilum 81-85
    illustrations 10, 25, 31, 73, 82,
    83, 136
Peristeria 80
Pescatorea 65
Pests 114-116
Petal 24-26
Phaius 15, 73
Phalaenopsis 70-74
    illustrations 19, 22, 25, 63, 68,
    109, 126, 133
Phragmipedium 65, 84
Plant structure 9-21
Pots and potting 47-53, 64-66
Problems 113-119
Propagation 101-111
    seeds 8, 106-108
    vegetative 101-106
Pseudobulb 13, 21

Renanthera 79, 104
Repotting, see Pots and Potting
Reproductive parts of flower 26-27
Rhizome 13
Rhynchostylis 79
Roots 14, 18

Scale insects, see Pests
Schomburgkia 65
Seedlings 108
Sepal 24-25
Sheath 14, 21
Slabs, see Containers
Sobralia 65
Sophrocattleya 60
Sophrolaeliocattleya 60
Sophronitis 60
Species, see Names
Stanhopea 43
Stem 17
Sunlight, see Light
Sympodial growth 11-21
    propagation 101-105

Telipogon 80
Temperature 33-35
Terrestrial orchids 98
Tree fern 49-50
Trichopilia 65
Tubs, see Containers

Vandaceous orchids 74-79
Vanda 74-79
    illustrations 19, 72, 103, 111
Ventilation 36-39
Virus, see Diseases

Watering 39-42

Paphiopedilum Claret Tree (Winston Churchill x John Dovan). Slipper orchids are popular houseplants and greenhouse plants because of their spectacular, long-lasting flowers and attractive foliage.